Interpreting the Synoptic Gospels

Guides to New Testament Exegesis
Scot McKnight, General Editor

Interpreting the Synoptic Gospels

Scot McKnight

BAKER BOOK HOUSE
Grand Rapids, Michigan 49516

Printed in the United States of America

Library of Congress Cataloging-in-Publication Data

McKnight, Scot.
    Interpreting the synoptic gospels.

    (Guides to New Testament exegesis ; 2)
    Bibliography: p.
    1. Bible.   N.T.   Gospels—Hermeneutics.   I. Title.
II. Series.
BS2555.2.M39   1988   226'.06'01   88-10502
ISBN 0-8010-6235-7

For Walt Liefeld

Christian Brother,
Teacher,
and
Esteemed Colleague

Contents

Editor's Preface

Four literary types (genres) comprise the New Testament: the Gospels, the Acts of the Apostles, the Letters, and, finally, the Apocalypse. Each genre is distinct, and, as has been made abundantly clear by contemporary scholars, each requires different sensitivities, principles, and methods of interpretation. Consequently, applying the same method to different genres will often lead to serious misunderstandings. Consequently, students need manuals that will introduce them both to the specific nature of a particular genre and to basic principles for exegeting that genre.

The Guides to New Testament Exegesis series has been specifically designed to meet this need. These guides have been written, not for specialists, but for college religion majors, seminarians, and pastors who have had at least one year of Greek. Methods and principles may change, but the language of the New Testament remains the same. God chose to speak to people in Greek; serious students of the New Testament must learn to love that language in order better to understand the Word of God.

These guides also have a practical aim. Each guide presents various views of scholars on particular issues. Yet the ultimate goal of each is to provide methods and principles for interpreting the New Testament. Abstract discussions have their proper place but not in this series; these guides are intended for concrete application to the New Testament text. Various scholars, specializing in given areas of New Testament study, offer students their own methods and principles for interpreting specific genres of the New Testament. Such diversity provides a broader perspective for the student. Each volume concludes with a bibliography of twenty essential works for further study.

Previously the point was made that different genres require different methods and principles. Therefore, a basic exegetical method which can be adapted to various genres is essential. Because of the inevitable overlap of procedures, an introductory volume to the series will cover the basic methods and principles for each genre. The individual exegetical guides will then introduce the student to more specific background procedures for that particular genre.

The vision for this series comes from Gordon Fee's introduction to New Testament exegesis.[1] Without minimizing the important contribution Fee has made to New Testament study, this series goes beyond what he has presented. It intends to develop, as it were, handbooks for each of the genres of the New Testament.[2]

Finally, this series is dedicated to our teachers and students, in thanksgiving and hope. Our prayer is that God may use these books to lead his people into truth, love, and peace.

Scot McKnight

---

1. *New Testament Exegesis: A Handbook for Students and Pastors* (Philadelphia: Westminster, 1983).

2. A helpful introduction to the various genres of the New Testament is D. E. Aune, *The New Testament in Its Literary Environment,* Library of Early Christianity (Philadelphia: Westminster, 1987).

Author's Preface

This brief manual of synoptic exegesis represents the culmination of what I have learned from many teachers, authors, students, and personal encounters with the synoptic Gospels. Source-minded students will undoubtedly detect these various traditions and my redaction of them.

I am deeply conscious of the debt I owe to my teachers, especially to Dr. W. L. Liefeld, Distinguished Professor of New Testament Exegesis at Trinity Evangelical Divinity School, who first taught me to love my synopsis and adore the Lord to whom it bears witness. To President K. M. Meyer and Dean W. C. Kaiser, Jr., I express my sincere appreciation for affording me such a generous opportunity for research and writing. My *Doktorvater*, Professor James D. G. Dunn (Durham), carefully read the entire manuscript and, in his patient and gracious manner, made suggestions that have greatly improved the final product.

For those students at Trinity who have asked penetrating questions and offered insightful suggestions, I am thankful. My graduate assistants, John Raymond and Steve Ratliff, merit special mention.

Thanks go to my colleagues, especially to Drs. G. R. Osborne and M. J. Harris, who, through reading various portions of this book or discussing it, have contributed in no small measure to its value. Dr. J. H. Sailhamer has enlightened me many times as to the literary nature of the Gospel narratives. I ask him to accept, as a peace offering, my appendix.

My life companion and best friend, Kristen, makes possible a life full of joy and love—and time to study! However, my children, Laura and Lukas, are not so magnanimous; because they ask me to join them in flute and Narnia sessions and Little League baseball games, completion of this book has been joyfully delayed. Finally, I pay tribute to my favorite troubadours, Michael Card and John Michael Talbot, for enveloping my study with worshipful praise.

Scot McKnight

Introduction

Careful study of the synoptic Gospels can be a life-transforming experience. Yet for many, such study is unexciting because they fail to take the required time, they simply do not know how to study the synoptic Gospels, or they do not have the necessary background to guide them through various passages. This book is intended to help students formulate principles and methods for studying the synoptic Gospels. It reflects but one student/teacher's approach though it also reflects the standard methods of the scholarly guild.

How does one exegete a passage in the synoptic Gospels? Although this question is vital, too few Bible study guides recognize the importance of adapting the process of hermeneutics to the type of literature (genre) one is studying.[1] Though there are undoubtedly many similarities between exegeting Romans and Mark, for

---

1. A fine introduction to New Testament exegesis that is sensitive to genre (although its treatment of each of the genre is too abbreviated) is G. D. Fee's *New Testament Exegesis: A Handbook for Students and Pastors* (Philadelphia: Westminster, 1983). Others of note include: W. Barclay, *An Introduction to the First Three Gospels*, rev. ed. (Philadelphia: Westminster, 1975); R. F. Collins, *Introduction to the New Testament* (Garden City: Doubleday, 1983); K. F. Nickle, *The Synoptic Gospels: Consensus and Conflict* (Atlanta: John Knox, 1980); R. H. Stein, *The Synoptic Problem: An Introduction* (Grand Rapids: Baker, 1987); J. B. Green, *How to Read the Gospels and Acts* (Downers Grove, Ill.: Inter-Varsity Press, 1987). For the broader discussion of the importance of genre, see K. J. Vanhoozer, "The Semantics of Biblical Literature: Truth and Scripture's Diverse Literary Forms," in *Hermeneutics, Authority, and Canon*, ed. by D. A. Carson and J. D. Woodbridge, 53–104 (Grand Rapids: Zondervan, 1986).

example, their genres are strikingly different. Romans is a logical and didactic letter that attempts to explicate the salvation accomplished in Christ. Mark, on the other hand, is a Gospel with a plot, point of view, events, and characters, as well as a prehistory. Because of these differences, anyone who applies precisely the same method of interpretation to both books will inevitably misunderstand at least one of them.

The synoptic Gospels are three-dimensional or evolutionary in character. Each contains both events and sayings purporting to be from Jesus' life; these events and sayings, however, were not recorded immediately in the Gospels but were instead transmitted through various means, the most notable of which were word of mouth and written collections. Thus, when we read the Gospels, we are reading about things spoken or done by Jesus, passed on by the early church through oral transmission and probably some written collections, and only later recorded in the Gospels. Consequently, any exegetical method which ignores any of the phases of a Gospel's development will shortchange the interpreter.

The transmission process is not the only thing that affects synoptic exegesis. Even the most casual reader will notice that both sayings and events occur in different settings in the Gospels (cf. Matt. 6:9–13, with Luke 11:2–4; cf. Matt. 12:1–8 with Mark 2:23–28), while others are situated in identical settings (cf. Matt. 15:1–16:12 with Mark 7:1–8:21). Some stories seem to be told from different perspectives (cf. Matt. 8:5–13 with Luke 7:1–10), whereas others are repeated almost verbatim (cf. Luke 6:1–5 with Mark 2:23–28; Matt. 23:37–39 with Luke 13:34–35). Such comparisons illustrate that not only have sayings and events been transmitted in both oral and written form, but that the Gospels are not strictly concerned with chronological biography.

The diverse methods used to analyze these various stages of transmission and the resultant product are collectively known as *Traditionsgeschichte* (tradition criticism). We will investigate these disciplines in greater detail in the chapters which follow, noting both their strengths and inherent weaknesses, but they need to be mentioned here by way of introduction (see table 1).

The entire discipline concerned with the development of the Gospels is called tradition criticism. This term is also used for the more "refined" process of determining by use of certain criteria what is authentic (historically reliable) in the Gospels. Whereas

Table 1

The Disciplines of Tradition Criticism
Transmission of Event or Saying

Event	Oral Traditions	Written Sources	Text
Tradition Criticism	Form Criticism	Source Criticism	Redaction Criticism
			Literary Criticism

Tradition Criticism

tradition criticism focuses on the original event, form criticism is concerned with the oral stage between that original event and the written, canonical record. Besides oral transmission, the early church also passed on traditions in written collections. The discipline which seeks to discover those written traditions behind the Gospels is called source criticism. The discipline of tradition history

Table 2

Basic Synoptic Exegesis
Preliminary Considerations

1. Introductory issues (author, provenance, structure, *Sitz im Leben*, etc.)
2. Background (social, religious, cultural, historical)
3. Relationship of the Gospels (Synoptic Problem)

Basic Synoptic Exegesis

Step	Goal
Textual analysis	Original text
Grammatical analysis	Grammatical relations, exegetical issues, preliminary translation, additional background study
Tradition-critical analysis	History of the pericope
Questions about Jesus	Judgments about history
Questions about forms	Judgments about oral transmission and literary forms behind the text
Questions about author's contributions	Judgments about author's primary concerns and redaction strategies
Word studies	Denotative/connotative meanings of significant words
Motif/thematic analysis	Author's theology
Translation	Explicative translation
Statement of intention	Author's aim for pericope

concerned with the written Gospels is called redaction criticism. This discipline seeks to determine from a written source the particular contributions of the final editor in order better to understand his theological point of view. (Literary criticism, only distantly related to the tradition-critical process, is also included in table 1.)

The exegete of the synoptic Gospels must recognize the important characteristics of the Gospels, particularly their three-dimensional nature. This book will take the student through the steps of synoptic exegesis (see table 2). Obviously, pastors will not be able to exhaust this process every time they prepare a sermon, but by learning the correct procedure and practicing it, they will know which shortcuts they can take in preparing a home Bible study or sermon, or in personal study.

Before proceeding to the various aspects of Gospel studies, it is helpful to remind ourselves of the purpose of exegesis. In general, the purpose of exegesis is to determine, with reasonable probability, the *intention of the author* as he has made that intention known *in the text in its historical context.*[2]

---

2. For defense of this definition, see E. D. Hirsch, Jr., *Validity in Interpretation* (New Haven, Conn.: Yale University Press, 1967); W. C. Kaiser, Jr., *Toward an Exegetical Theology: Biblical Exegesis for Preaching and Teaching* (Grand Rapids: Baker, 1981), 23–36.

Part 1

Preliminary Steps
of Synoptic Exegesis

1

Introductory Questions

Students of the Gospels are probably least interested in introductory questions dealing with authorship, provenance, and *Sitz im Leben*. This disinterest is unfortunate since the results of these issues affect, however subtly, the exegesis of a large number of passages.

In examining introductory issues, students will encounter discussions about the authorship, date, provenance (origin), structure, and *Sitz im Leben* of a given Gospel. Some issues are unique to a particular Gospel (e.g., the text-critical problem in Mark). In this chapter, we shall look briefly at the basic issues affecting synoptic exegesis. However, before briefly examining these introductory questions, some recommendations are necessary.

Preliminary Recommendations

Each student should own the following introductions. The standard evangelical work is D. Guthrie's *New Testament Introduction*.[1] Guthrie includes a comprehensive survey of various positions and the evidence used for each position taken; the bibliographies, though somewhat dated, remain useful. W. G. Kümmel's *Introduc-*

---

1. D. Guthrie, *New Testament Introduction*, 3d ed. (Downers Grove, Ill.: Inter-Varsity Press, 1970).

tion to the New Testament represents a contrasting perspective.[2] A
mediating view is expressed by R. P. Martin in *New Testament Foundations: A Guide for Christian Students.*[3] It is imperative that the student read introductions written by scholars representing different
viewpoints in order to grasp the issues more fully. In addition,
students should also peruse introductions to the Gospels in three
or four standard critical commentaries (see the Selected Bibliography).

How, then, should one approach introductory issues? Frequently, a student reads an introduction and simply accepts what
he or she has read. Or the student reads several introductions and
commentaries, and then assumes the most tenable position. Finally, the student may read introductions and commentaries, carefully scrutinize the arguments and evidence presented by each
author, and then compose a brief introduction to each Gospel for
reference (and later revision when other material is read). The latter
approach is recommended.

Introductory Questions

Authorship and Date

The names of the synoptic authors (Matthew, Mark, and Luke)
are almost certainly not original to the text itself. Rather, they were
probably added by later scribes who, perhaps with solid evidence,
decided not to leave the authors anonymous.[4]

If this is the case, then it would be wise for evangelicals to refrain
from insisting that conclusions regarding authorship are simply a
matter of conservative versus liberal interpretation; if the inscrip-

---

2. W. G. Kümmel, *Introduction to the New Testament*, trans. by H. C. Kee
(Nashville: Abingdon, 1975).

3. R. P. Martin, *New Testament Foundations: A Guide for Christian Students.* 2
vols. (Grand Rapids: Eerdmans, 1975, 1978).

4. That the authors' names were added later is the scholarly consensus.
However, it should be noted that we possess no extant texts that omit the
author's name. The fact that various titles are found in the manuscript tradition
supports the view that the names were added later.

tions are later additions then they are not inspired and may be inaccurate.

In determining the authorship and date of a particular Gospel, students need to consider internal evidence (what the Gospel itself says about authorship and/or date), external evidence (what the early church has preserved), and comparative evidence (the relationship of the Synoptics).

An important consideration in this connection is the slippery logic often used by conservative evangelicals when discussing authorship. The standard approach is as follows:

Early church tradition affirms Luke as the author.

Liberal arguments contrary to this affirmation are lacking.

Therefore, Luke wrote the Gospel of Luke.

What such logic demonstrates is that the arguments against Lukan authorship are not compelling; it does not prove that Luke actually wrote the Gospel. This logic also demonstrates that there is nothing that disproves the tradition of the early church. However, irrefutable evidence for traditional authorship is difficult to find. One might be able to disprove antitraditional views and muster evidence which confirms Luke's authorship (medical concerns and language), but it must be admitted, even by conservative evangelicals, that the evidence for traditional authorship consists solely of early church testimony.[5] However, just because Luke's authorship is affirmed only by the early church fathers does not imply that it is inaccurate. In order clearly to disprove that ascription, positive evidence must be offered which grants credence to another. In the lack of solid evidence it is better to admit ignorance than to argue for another author.

If we can determine with reasonable probability that a given author wrote a Gospel, then we also have a good clue as to its date. Even in cases where a scholar contends that traditional authorship is either impossible to validate or remains undetermined, legitimate

---

5. The second appendix of K. Aland's *Synopsis Quattuor Evangeliorum*, 10th ed. (Stuttgart: Deutsche Bibelgesellschaft, 1978), is an anthology of important statements made by the early church on authorship. See esp. 531–48.

inferences as to date can be made (e.g., that Matt. 22:7 reflects a post–A.D. 70 setting).

Provenance

The provenance (origin) of the Gospels, like authorship, is a matter about which little consensus has been reached. There are basically two kinds of evidence for provenance: external (comments found in early church writings) and internal (inferences from the text). The earliest writings (external evidence) usually associate Matthew with Palestine and both Mark and Luke with Rome. As far as internal evidence, two examples must suffice. Some scholars contend that persecution references (8:34–38; 10:38–39; 13:9–13) and Latinisms (4:21; 5:9, 15; 6:27) in the Gospel of Mark point to Rome as its likely place of origin, while the mention of two drach-mae might point toward Antioch in the case of Matthew (that was the value of the temple tax there; see Matt. 17:24–27). However, inferences like these must be weighed carefully before being used for exegetical decisions.

Sitz im Leben

The German expression *Sitz im Leben* ("occasion," "setting in life") is used frequently in Gospel studies. Like authorship and provenance, the precise *Sitz im Leben* of the Gospels cannot be determined conclusively; consequently, a multitude of theories has been articulated for each Gospel.

Generally, *Sitz im Leben* theorists conclude that the Gospels were written: (1) to meet liturgical needs; (2) to settle polemical issues (either within or outside the Christian community); (3) to provide information about Jesus; (4) to instruct new converts in Christian living; or (5) to evangelize nonbelievers. Scholars are usually led to these conclusions on the basis of inference from distinctive or characteristic tendencies in one Gospel. The problem is distinguishing a tendency from an accurate report about Jesus.

Such theories, while worthy of the student's attention, are so speculative that they should not be utilized as a hermeneutical grid through which every pericope in a Gospel is filtered. Valuable as they might be, *Sitz im Leben* studies are best left as suggestive conclusions at the end, rather than the beginning, of a commentary.[6]

Structure

The structure of a Gospel is not subject to such speculative difficulties. A proposal for the structure of a book is nothing other than an attempt to outline the whole of a Gospel in order to make sense of its individual pericopes. In composing such an outline, a student may choose to consult a commentary or an introduction and simply copy an outline without personal reflection. The more advanced student may examine the proposals in several introductions and commentaries and then choose the most compelling structural outline. A third approach, followed by the serious student, is a careful examination of several introductions and the standard commentaries, accompanied by intense study of the Gospel, until a satisfactory proposal of structure has been obtained.

It is necessary for the student to work through the Gospels individually to determine the structure of each because such a procedure will greatly aid the exegesis and future study of them. The following procedure is suggested:

1. In the first column, list every paragraph in the Gospel by chapter and verse.
2. Read through the Gospel, and give a simple summary of each paragraph in the second column.
3. Use additional columns to give general descriptions of larger units.

For example, Matthew 1:1–2:23 constitutes the prologue to the Gospel. Simple summaries of a pericope are listed on the left; more general structural descriptions of larger units occur on the right. (A basic outline will eventually appear in the far right margin.)

After completing an outline, the student should read the structural proposals of scholars, using at least three good introductions and commentaries. At this stage, the student should interact with

---

6. Some insightful comments regarding such theories and their dubious value for interpretation are articulated by B. S. Childs, *The New Testament as Canon: An Introduction* (Philadelphia: Fortress, 1985), 57–116, 480–87.

Table 3

Structural Proposals for the Gospel of Mark*

	Chapters 1	2	3	4	5	6	7	8	9	10	11	12	13	14	15	16
A. Plummer	1:1–13 Introduction	1:14 Galilee and Neighborhood							9:50	10 Journey to Jerusalem	11:1 Last Work in Jerusalem				15:41	15:42–16:8 Conclusion
H. B. Swete	1:1–13 Prologue	1:14 The Ministry in Galilee							9:50	10 Judean & Peraean Journeys	11:1 The Last Week at Jerusalem					16:8
V. Taylor	1:1–13 Introduction	1:14 The Galilean Ministry	3:6	3:7 The Height of the Galilean Ministry		6:13	6:14 The Ministry Beyond Galilee	8:26	8:27 Caesarea Philippi: The Journey to Jerusalem	10:52	11:1 The Ministry in Jerusalem		13:37	14:1 The Passion & Resurrection Narrative		16:8
C. Cranfield	1:1–13 Beginning	1:14 Begin. of the Galilean Ministry	3:6	3:7 Later Stages of the Galilean Ministry		6:13	6:14 Jesus Goes Outside Galilee	8:26	8:27 The Way to Jerusalem	10:52	11:1 Ministry in Jerusalem		13:37	14:1 The Passion	15:47	16:8 The Resurrection

	1:1–13	1:14	3:6	3:7	6:6a / 6:13 / 5:43	6:6b / 6:14 / 6:1	8:26	8:27	10:52 / 10:45	11:1	12:44	13	14:1	15:47	16:1-8
D. E. Nineham	Prologue	The Galilean Ministry						From Gal. to Jer.: The Character of Jesus		The Ministry in Jerusalem		Future Foretold	The Passion of Christ		The Resurrection
E. Schweizer	Beginning	Authority of Jesus & Blind. of . . .		Jesus' Ministry in Parables & Signs and the . . .		Jesus' Ministry to the Gentiles & the Blindness . . .		Jesus' Open Revelation & the Meaning . . .		The Passion & the Resurrection of the Son of Man (to 16:8)					
W. L. Lane	Prologue	Initial Phase of Gal. Min.		Later Phases of the Ministry in Galilee		Withdrawal Beyond Galilee (6:14–8:30)		The Journey to Jerusalem (8:31–)		Ministry in Jerusalem (to 13:37)			The Passion Narrative		The Resurrection
V. Robbins	Introduction	Jesus & the gospel of God		The Healing Son of God		The Rejected Prophet		The Suffering, Dying, Rising Son of Man (to 10:45)		The Authoritative Son of David (10:46–12:44)		The Future Son of Man & the Dying Messiah-King (13:1–)			Conclusion

*This sampling of the structural proposals for Mark was prepared by my graduate assistant, Stephen A. Ratliff.

1:1–17	Genealogy	Genealogy		Genealogy	Prologue
1:18–25	Birth	OT Prophecy re: Name		OT Prophecies	
2:1–12	Magi	OT Prophecy re: Place			
2:13–15	Flight	OT Prophecy re: Flight			
2:16–18	Rachel	OT Prophecy re: Threats			
2:19–23	Nazareth	OT Prophecy re: Residence			

the various positions and gradually arrive at a structural proposal which is both personal and conversant with the major scholarly positions. Because scholarly opinions on this matter are often quite different, some comments about organizing these proposals are in order.

One way of cataloguing various proposals is to follow this procedure:

1. List the scholars, in chronological order, in the right margin of a page.
2. List the chapters of the Gospel across the top of the page.
3. Mark each scholar's divisions of that Gospel at the appropriate point in the chart.

If a wide sheet of paper is used, the scholar's descriptions for the major divisions may be written in the chart. In doing this, especially if the scholars are listed in chronological order, the student can readily observe the major positions as well as the history of research. Table 3 provides an example of such a chart.

By carefully examining this chart, one can readily see that there is some unanimity among scholars in the ordering of Mark. (Only rarely should students differ radically from the majority of scholars.)

We have investigated some preliminary issues affecting exegesis, namely, authorship, provenance, *Sitz im Leben*, and structure. Before discussing the basic steps of exegesis, background studies and the relationship of the synoptic Gospels must be examined.

2

Background Considerations

The student's knowledge of the ancient world greatly affects exegesis. Just as it is important to have certain "interpretative grids" in our minds as we read the *Chicago Tribune* or Allan Bloom's *Closing of the American Mind*, so it is crucial for the New Testament student to be able to think like first-century Jews, to hear their expressions, to share their customs, and to experience their social milieu. Yet "background" does not imply that we need to know everything about the ancient world before we can comprehend the Gospels. In fact, the process is a circular one: as we understand more about the Gospels, we understand more about that world; and as we understand more about that world, so we understand more about the Gospels.

Background considerations are necessary if the student is to uncover elements in the text that were simply assumed by the first-century writer and his audience in order to understand the intention of the author as made known in the text. By the original author and his readers, this knowledge was shared; due to historical distance, this information is arcane to us. And there is much the Gospel traveler will need to know in order to be a perceptive visitor in that world.[1]

In this connection, discipline is necessary in background studies. The student must limit investigation to that which is pertinent

---

1. An excellent introduction to the ancient world (sources and history) is E. Ferguson's *Backgrounds of Early Christianity* (Grand Rapids: Eerdmans, 1987).

for interpretation. For example, if one decides to investigate the nature and purpose of genealogies (e.g., Matt. 1:1–17), one may become overwhelmed in the attempt to access all available sources (e.g., Jewish historians and philosophers [Josephus, Philo, 1 Macc.] to determine the importance of heritage and geographical, political, and religious connections, in addition to pertinent Old Testament passages). One's quest, particularly in the context of sermon preparation, must be much more narrow and will probably be limited to a few dictionary articles and the exegesis of a few relevant passages elsewhere in the Bible. In that every topic is a potential doctoral dissertation, the student must learn to discard what is not directly pertinent.

Obviously, thorough background study provides historical anchoring. The student who is familiar with a Jewish perspective on table fellowship will understand the implications of Matthew 9:9–13. The student who knows nothing about the Maccabean revolt will fail to recognize why the Jews were so upset by Jesus' and Paul's attitudes toward the Law and temple. Interpretation which is not anchored in background studies will be historically insensitive and, therefore, simply wrong. Christians who neglect background information are in danger of denying the time-conditioned nature of revelation, both in the event and in the text.

As mentioned above, the problem with background studies is that they can prove infeasible for pastors. Therefore, basic sources must be mastered for quick reference to solid and responsible facts. Again, there are basically three ways to approach background studies: (1) read the original sources (Old Testament, Apocrypha, pseudepigrapha, New Testament, Graeco-Roman sources, rabbis) and conduct an inductive study [this will take several years]; (2) peruse general surveys in standard reference works; (3) consult the best surveys, then examine the evidence. Using the latter approach, the student can become a sensitive historian.

Too few students have read Josephus, and fewer still have studied Philo, the Dead Sea Scrolls, or the rabbinical writings. Such neglect results in interpretations that are anachronistic and misleading. It is my recommendation that every seminary student, before graduation, should read the Old Testament Apocrypha, the Manual of Discipline (the Dead Sea Scrolls), Josephus's *Jewish War*, 1 Enoch, Jubilees, the Sibylline Oracles, the Odes and Psalms of Solomon, the Testaments of the Twelve Patriarchs, the Babylonian

Talmud (at least five Mishnah tractates [including Aboth] with commentary), the Gospel of Thomas, and portions of the Graeco-Roman literature (Plato's *Republic*, Aristotle's *Ethics*, Suetonius's *Augustus*, Tacitus's *Annals*, as well as some papyrii and inscriptions). At the very minimum, the student should read C. K. Barrett's *The New Testament Background: Selected Documents*.[2] Someone who possesses both ability and opportunity and who has not read this minimal amount of material is frankly unprepared for interpretation and insensitive to the task of New Testament exegesis.

Many introductions to the original sources have been written. A good place to begin is E. Schürer's *The History of the Jewish People in the Age of Jesus Christ*.[3] Other introductions can be found in encyclopediae and individual editions and volumes.

The following is a list of basic primary and secondary background sources. The inexperienced exegete should spend at least an hour in each category of secondary literature, perusing these works, as well as locate and read selections from each of the major primary sources.

Primary Sources and Concordances

Old Testament

Elliger, W., and W. Rudolph. *Biblia Hebraica Stuttgartensia*. Stuttgart: Deutsche Bibelstiftung, 1977.

Even-Shoshan, A. *A New Concordance of the Old Testament*. Introduction by J. H. Sailhamer. Grand Rapids: Baker, 1984.

Hatch, E., and H. A. Redpath. *A Concordance to the Septuagint*. 2 vols. Grand Rapids: Baker, 1983. Includes Old Testament Apocrypha.

Rahlffs, A. *Septuaginta*. New York: United Bible Societies, 1965.

Pseudepigrapha

Charlesworth, J. H. *The Old Testament Pseudepigrapha*. 2 vols. New York: Doubleday, 1983, 1985.

---

2. C. K. Barrett, *The New Testament Background: Selected Documents* (San Francisco: Harper & Row, 1961).

3. E. Schürer, *The History of the Jewish People in the Age of Jesus Christ* (Edinburgh: T. & T. Clark, 1973), 1:17–122.

No complete concordance is available; see C. A. Wahl, *Clavis Librorum Veteris Testamenti Apocryphorum Philologica* (Graz, Austria: Akademische Druck, 1972).

Dead Sea Scrolls

Barthelemy, D., et al. *Discoveries in the Judean Desert.* Multivolume. Oxford: Oxford University Press, 1955–   .

Kuhn, K. G. *Konkordanz zu den Qumrantexten.* Göttingen: Vandenhoeck & Ruprecht, 1960. Updated in various fascicles of *Revue de Qumran.*

Lohse, E. *Die Texte aus Qumran.* Munich: Kösel, 1971. Hebrew edition of the major sectarian scrolls with German translation and pointing.

Vermes, G. *The Dead Sea Scrolls in English.* 2d ed. London: Penguin, 1975. Omits lines.

Philo

Mayer, G. *Index Philoneus.* Berlin and New York: Walter de Gruyter, 1974.

Philo. *Philosophical Works.* Loeb Classical Library. 12 vols. Cambridge, Mass.: Harvard University Press, 1927–1962.

Josephus

Josephus. *Life, Against Apion, Jewish War, Jewish Antiquities.* Loeb Classical Library. 10 vols. Cambridge, Mass.: Harvard University Press, 1926–1965.

Rengstorf, K. H. *A Complete Concordance to Flavius Josephus.* 5 vols. Leiden: E. J. Brill, 1973–1983.

Rabbis

Blackman, P. *Mishnayot: Pointed Hebrew Text.* 7 vols. New York: Judaica Press, 1964.

Danby, H. *The Mishnah.* London: Oxford University Press, 1933.

Epstein, I. *The Babylonian Talmud.* 34 vols. London: Soncino, 1935–1952.

Neusner, J. *The Tosefta.* 6 vols. New York: Ktav, 1977–   .

Zuckermandel, M. S. *Tosephta.* Jerusalem: Wahrmann, 1970.

About Judaism

Holladay, C. R. *Fragments from Hellenistic Jewish Authors*. Vol. 1, *Historians*. Chico, Calif.: Scholars Press, 1983.

Stern, M. *Greek and Latin Authors on Jews and Judaism*. 2 vols. Jerusalem: Israel Academy of Sciences and Humanities, 1974, 1980.

Secondary Sources

Historical Background

Bruce, F. F. *New Testament History*. New York: Doubleday, 1972.

Cohen, S. J. D. *From the Maccabees to the Mishnah*. Library of Early Christianity. Philadelphia: Westminster, 1987. A useful introduction to the emergence of Christianity and rabbinic Judaism.

Ferguson, E. *Backgrounds of Early Christianity*. Grand Rapids: Eerdmans, 1987. Includes detailed bibliographies.

Hengel, M. *Judaism & Hellenism: Studies in Their Encounter in Palestine During the Early Hellenistic Period*. Philadelphia: Fortress, 1974. A model study of the interpenetration of Hellenism and Judaism. An updated summary is *Jews, Greeks and Barbarians: Aspects of the Hellenization of Judaism in the Pre-Christian Period* (Philadelphia: Fortress, 1980).

Hoehner, H. *Herod Antipas*. Grand Rapids: Zondervan, 1980.

Koester, H. *History, Culture and Religion of the Hellenistic Age*. Philadelphia: Fortress, 1982.

Schürer, E. *The History of the Jewish People in the Age of Jesus Christ, 175 B.C.–A.D. 135*. Revised and edited by G. Vermes and F. Millar. 4 vols. Edinburgh: T. & T. Clark, 1973, 1979, 1986, 1987.

Cultural/Religious/Social Background

Jeremias, J. *Jerusalem in the Time of Jesus*. Philadelphia: Fortress, 1969.

————. *New Testament Theology: The Proclamation of Jesus*. New York: Charles Scribner's Sons, 1971.

Safrai, S., et al. *The Jewish People in the First Century*. 4 vols. Philadelphia: Fortress, 1974, 1976, 1985–   .

Sanders, E. P. *Paul and Palestinian Judaism: A Comparison of Patterns of Religion*. Philadelphia: Fortress, 1977.

Urbach, E. E. *The Sages.* 2 vols. Jerusalem: Magnes, 1975. Rabbinic theology.

Helpful works in this area include the standard encyclopediae and word studies such as G. Kittel, *Theological Dictionary of the New Testament* (Grand Rapids: Eerdmans, 1976).

Literary Background

Aune, D. E. *The New Testament in Its Literary Environment.* Library of Early Christianity. Philadelphia: Westminster, 1987.

Bultmann, R. *The History of the Synoptic Tradition.* Translated by J. Marsh. San Francisco: Harper & Row, 1963. A categorization of the various forms utilized in the Gospels.

Gundry, R. H. "Recent Investigations into the Literary Genre 'Gospel.'" In *New Dimensions in New Testament Study,* edited by R. N. Longenecker and M. C. Tenney, 97–114. Grand Rapids: Zondervan, 1974.

Stanton, G. N. *Jesus of Nazareth in New Testament Preaching.* Society for New Testament Studies Monograph Series, no. 27. Cambridge: Cambridge University Press, 1974. A critique of form criticism.

Talbert, C. H. *What Is a Gospel?* Philadelphia: Fortress, 1977. A demonstration of the biographical nature of the Gospels.

3

The Synoptic Problem

The final preliminary issue affecting exegesis of the Synoptics is the relationship of these Gospels (the Synoptic Problem). Accordingly, in this chapter we will briefly outline some major solutions to the Synoptic Problem, argue for Markan priority, and then discuss the procedure for underlining a synopsis.[1]

The Biblical Warrant for Source Criticism

The Synoptic Problem is concerned with the literary relationship of Matthew, Mark, and Luke to each other as well as certain hypothetical sources. Comparing Matthew 14:22–33 and Mark 6:45–52, for example, one notices that Matthew has a long section, not found in Mark, about Peter's attempt to walk on the water. Furthermore, both stories end in surprisingly different ways: Mark's on a rather critical note, Matthew's on a confessional beat. If one argues that

---

1. Several good synopses are available. The standard text is K. Aland (ed.), *Synopsis Quattuor Evangeliorum,* 10th ed. (Stuttgart: Deutsche Bibelstiftung, 1978). See also A. Huck and H. Greeven, *Synopsis of the First Three Gospels,* 13th ed. (Tübingen: J. C. B. Mohr [Paul Siebeck], 1981); J. B. Orchard, *A Synopsis of the Four Gospels in Greek, Arranged According to the Two-Gospel Hypothesis* (Macon, Ga.: Mercer University Press, 1983). For comparison of the modern synopses, see J. K. Elliott, "An Examination of the Text and Apparatus of Three Recent Greek Synopses," *New Testament Studies* 32 (1986): 557–82; K. Aland, *The Text of the New Testament* (Grand Rapids: Eerdmans, 1987), 256–62.

Matthew is dependent upon Mark, the incident involving Peter and the more confessional conclusion are notable additions. However, if one argues that Mark has used Matthew, then why Mark has omitted the episode about Peter and changed a confessional statement into a criticism is intriguing.

However valuable a solution to the Synoptic Problem may be, the data are nevertheless exceedingly complex and scholars have not obtained consensus.[2] Source criticism attempts to identify the written traditions behind the Gospels in order to determine the relationship of the Synoptics. A good place to look carefully at this discipline is Luke 1:1–4.

Luke tells us clearly that there were *many other gospels* in existence when he wrote (πολλοὶ ἐπεχείρησαν ἀνατάξασθαι διήγησιν, "*many* have attempted to narrate an account/compose a narrative" [1:1]). These narratives reflected earlier oral traditions (καθὼς παρέδοσαν ἡμῖν οἱ ἀπ᾽ ἀρχῆς αὐτόπται καὶ ὑπηρέται γενόμενοι τοῦ λόγου, "just as those who were eyewitnesses from the beginning and servants of the word had *passed* [*them*] *on to us*" [1:2]). Luke explicitly states that he consulted other sources in writing his Gospel. He numbers himself among the many and decides to *investigate his sources and write an orderly account* (1:3): ἔδοξε κἀμοὶ παρηκολουθηκότι ἄνωθεν πᾶσιν ἀκριβῶς καθεξῆς σοι γράψαι ("and, since I have followed everything from the beginning very carefully, it seemed good to me to write to you an orderly account" [1:3]). Since Luke operated in this manner, it is reasonable to surmise that the other Gospel writers must have used the same procedure. Source criticism attempts to ascertain, where possible, the sources of the

---

2. For helpful overviews of the Synoptic Problem, see A. J. Bellinzoni, Jr. (ed.), *The Two-Source Hypothesis: A Critical Appraisal* (Macon, Ga.: Mercer University Press, 1985); S. Neill, *The Interpretation of the New Testament, 1861–1961* (London: Oxford University Press, 1964), 104–27; C. M. Tuckett, *The Revival of the Griesbach Hypothesis: An Analysis and Appraisal*, Society for New Testament Monograph Series, no. 44 (Cambridge: Cambridge University Press, 1983). Two works which argue for the Griesbach Hypothesis are W. R. Farmer, *The Synoptic Problem: A Critical Analysis* (Dillsboro, N.C.: Western North Carolina Press, 1976 [1964]); and H.-H. Stoldt, *History and Criticism of the Marcan Hypothesis* (Macon, Ga.: Mercer University Press, 1980). A recent defense of the Markan hypothesis is R. H. Stein, *The Synoptic Problem: An Introduction* (Grand Rapids: Baker, 1987). I am grateful to Dr. Stein for allowing me to use his manuscript prior to publication.

Evangelists in order to understand their intentions. However, whereas source criticism seems demanded both by the statement in Luke and the observations which will confront the reader while underlining, a solution to the Synoptic Problem is not so easily discerned. To these various solutions we must now turn.

Major Solutions to the Synoptic Problem

The Augustinian Hypothesis

Augustine's solution to the Synoptic Problem was that Matthew was first, Mark used Matthew, and Luke was last, using both Matthew and Mark: "Now, those four evangelists . . . are believed to have written in the order which follows: first Matthew, then Mark, thirdly Luke, lastly John"; "Mark follows him [Matthew] closely, and looks like his attendant and epitomizer."[3] For Augustine, the canonical order is the chronological order. Thus: Matthew–Mark–Luke.

The Griesbach Hypothesis

J. J. Griesbach is recognized for his work in textual criticism. However, he also addressed the Synoptic Problem. Although his view was championed by many initially, it is now held by few; it has been defended most vociferously of late by W. R. Farmer. Basically, the Griesbach Hypothesis maintains that Matthew was first; Luke, using Matthew, was second; Mark was last and used both Matthew and Luke. Thus: Matthew–Luke–Mark.

The Oxford Hypothesis

The Oxford Hypothesis, also called the Two-/Four-Source Hypothesis, is held by most New Testament scholars, and is assumed

---

3. Augustine, *Harmony of the Gospels*, Nicene and Post-Nicene Fathers, ed. P. Schaff (Grand Rapids: Eerdmans, 1979), vol. 6, 1.2.3, 1.2.4, respectively. Recently this view of Augustine has been challenged. See D. Peabody, "Augustine and the Augustinian Hypothesis: A Reexamination of Augustine's Thought in *De consensu evangelistarum*," in W. R. Farmer, ed., *New Synoptic Studies: The Cambridge Conference and Beyond*, 37–64 (Macon, Ga.: Mercer Univ. Press, 1983).

in almost every major reference work. B. H. Streeter presents the standard statement of this position.[4] Even though his hypothesis is outdated in several aspects, it remains a classic and students should work through at least part 2. W. Sanday's *Studies in the Synoptic Problem by Members of the University of Oxford*[5] is an anthology of studies by members of the editor's Gospel Seminar, which met nine times per year for approximately sixteen years. It reflects the time when the Synoptic Problem was being recognized and a basic solution was forged.

The Oxford Hypothesis holds that Mark was first; Matthew was second and used Mark and Q; Luke was last and used Mark and Q. Both Matthew and Luke each had access to another source (M and L, respectively). Thus, there are four sources: Mark, Q, M, L. Some scholars prefer a Two-Source Hypothesis, seeing Mark and Q as the fundamental sources with M and L merely representing the sayings and events peculiar to Matthew and Luke, respectively.

That Markan priority dominates synoptic exegesis today is acknowledged by A. J. Bellinzoni: "Since Markan priority is an assumption of so much of the research of the last century, many of the conclusions of that research would have to be redrawn and much of the literature rewritten if the consensus of scholarship were suddenly to shift."[6]

The Farrer Hypothesis

Several scholars, while accepting Markan priority, reject Q and argue that Luke used Matthew instead. This view is particularly associated with Austin Farrer.[7] Its basic solution: Mark–Matthew–Luke.

Though these are the most popular solutions to the Synoptic Problem, it should not be supposed that each has had an equal

---

4. B. H. Streeter, *The Four Gospels: A Study of Origins* (London: Macmillan, 1924).

5. W. Sanday, *Studies in the Synoptic Problem by Members of the University of Oxford* (Oxford: Clarendon, 1911).

6. Bellinzoni, *Two-Source Hypothesis*, 9.

7. A. Farrer, "On Dispensing with Q," in *Studies in the Gospels: Essays in Memory of R. H. Lightfoot*, ed. by D. E. Nineham, 55–88 (Oxford: Basil Blackwell, 1955).

number of adherents. In fact, the numbers are overwhelmingly in favor of the Oxford Hypothesis. Since Streeter, no other theory has commanded such scholarly attention until the last two decades, when the Griesbach theory has had some vocal proponents.

Defense of the Oxford Hypothesis

While not discounting the difficulties of the Oxford Hypothesis or the strengths of the other views, according to the majority of scholars today, the Oxford Hypothesis (Markan priority) is the most tenable solution to the Synoptic Problem.

In examining the Synoptic Problem, one needs to make a clear distinction between the *phenomena* which cannot be disputed (e.g., that Matthew, Mark, and Luke often report the same event in identical words) and a hypothesis, or *explanation*, of those facts (e.g., Matthew and Luke both used Mark). We now need to look at the phenomena. First, one needs to observe the fact of similar content among the Synoptics: 90 percent of the contents of Mark are found in Matthew and 53 percent occur in Luke. (Griesbach proponents judiciously maintain that the previous statement is presumptuous because it can be expressed in the reverse order.) Furthermore, the Gospel writers often use similar or identical wording for the same material. Thus, for example, much of Mark's wording is found in Luke. There is also similar ordering of both content and wording. In fact, "whenever Matthew's order and Mark's order differ, Mark's order and Luke's order agree; and whenever Luke's order and Mark's order differ, Matthew's order and Mark's order agree."[8] That is to say, whenever Matthew or Luke diverge from Mark's order, they never agree against Mark in order of events. That is, if Luke departs from Mark's order, Matthew does not follow Luke (and vice versa). Similarities in content, wording, and order are the facts of the Synoptic Problem that need to be explained. In particular, similarity of order has led many scholars to the nearly

---

8. C. M. Tuckett, "Arguments from Order: Definition and Evaluation," in *Synoptic Studies: The Ampleforth Conferences of 1982 and 1983*, Journal for the Study of the New Testament-Supplement Series, no. 7, 198 (Sheffield: JSOT, 1984).

unanimous conclusion that the Synoptics are interdependent at the literary level.

Second, these phenomena admit to several explanations but one thing is virtually certain: Mark is somehow the crucial factor. Whether Mark was used by Matthew and Luke (Markan priority), or Matthew wrote and was used by Mark who was in turn used by Luke, or Matthew and Luke wrote prior to Mark and Mark used both, at some literary level Mark is the crucial factor. The question remains as to whether there are any substantial reasons for preferring one of these three solutions as more probable than the others.

Third, four decisive factors point specifically toward Markan priority.

1. It is standard procedure in New Testament textual criticism to prefer as original the "more primitive reading." G. D. Fee has argued the case for Markan priority on similar grounds.[9] Mark's style, more primitive than either Matthew's or Luke's, has been the decisive factor tipping the balance in favor of Markan priority.[10] (I note here that this argument is both crucial and complex but the details do emerge from a careful underlining of the synopsis). In general, while it is relatively easy to explain Matthew's and Luke's grammatical and stylistic changes of Mark, it is virtually impossible to explain Mark's grammar and style as a revision of Matthew's and Luke's.

2. Another important text-critical argument is that texts tend to expand rather than to shrink. Matthew and Luke are longer

---

9. G. D. Fee, "A Text-Critical Look at the Synoptic Problem," *Novum Testamentum* 22 (1980): 12–28.

10. See Stein, *Synoptic Problem*, 52–62; J. C. Hawkins, *Horae Synopticae: Contributions to the Study of the Synoptic Problem*, 2d ed. (Grand Rapids: Baker, 1968), 114–53; Streeter, *Four Gospels*, 162–64. If one can more easily explain Matthew and/or Luke changing Mark than the reverse, then it follows that Mark is prior (on text-critical grounds). An example can be found in Mark 2:18 (cf. Matt. 9:14; Luke 5:33). Mark is ambiguous about the questioners while Matthew and Luke are forthright. Is it more likely that Mark made the text ambiguous (*lectio difficilior*) or that Matthew and Luke made it more clear? On text-critical grounds the latter solution is preferred. Other examples can be found by comparing Mark with Matthew and Luke at Mark 1:12; 2:4; 4:41; 5:9–10; and 16:6.

than Mark, this tendency most clearly demonstrated in the birth narratives (see Matt. 1–2; Luke 1–2).

3. Scholars also argue that, at the level of the entire Gospel, given Matthew and Luke, it is hard to account for the need to have Mark—90 percent of Markan material is not new, and what is new is hardly innovative or necessary. On the other hand, they argue that, given Mark, it is relatively easy to account for the need for Matthew and Luke since both develop Mark in different ways with different additions and subtractions.

4. Redaction-critical studies endorse Markan priority simply because this hypothesis most satisfactorily explains the data. For example, Matthew's elimination of Mark's "harder readings" can easily be explained redactionally; in contrast, Mark's addition of "harder readings" is difficult to explain (cf. Mark 6:5–6 and Matt. 13:58; Mark 10:18 and Matt. 19:17). Recent redaction-critical studies of Matthew and Luke that assume Markan priority (e.g., J. A. Fitzmyer's commentary on Luke) demonstrate this argument.[11]

Fourth, it is probable that Matthew and Luke are independent and that, therefore, both Gospel writers used a certain source (Q) independently. (The letter Q is used rather loosely simply to designate the material common to Matthew and Luke; it cannot be demonstrated that Q was a complete gospel or that all of it was common at the written level.[12])

There are approximately two hundred verses, preponderantly sayings of Jesus, common to both Matthew and Luke which are not found in Mark; furthermore, the degree of similarity in wording in many of these pericopes, though not always identical (cf. Matt. 10:38–39; Luke 14:26–27; 17:33), is striking (cf. Matt. 3:7–10; Luke 3:7–9). There are arguments for the independence of Matthew and

---

11. Stein, *Synoptic Problem*, 76–86.

12. Excellent works on Q studies are Bellinzoni, *Two-Source Hypothesis*, 219–433; A. Polag, *Fragmenta Q: Textheft zur Logienquelle*, 2d ed. (Neukirchen: Neukirchener, 1982). Polag provides the scholarly consensus on the reconstruction of Q. The left pages contain the consensus text of Q; on the right pages, Polag provides an apparatus using various scholarly opinions in lieu of manuscript support. See also Stein, *Synoptic Problem*, 89–112.

Luke. If Luke and Matthew were largely dependent upon each other, one would expect, for example, that after the temptation there would be agreement in the placement of Jesus' sayings; but there is not. If they were dependent, one would expect that one of the authors would be consistently more Semitic than the other, but the fact is that sometimes Matthew and sometimes Luke preserve what is considered to be the more Semitic form of a saying of Jesus. Others have argued that it would be unlikely that Luke would shatter a masterpiece—the Sermon on the Mount—or that, when copying Mark, he would never pick up Matthew's additions. Thus, one could conclude that, if Matthew and Luke are independent and yet contain so many passages with such striking similarity in wording, then it is reasonable to conclude that both were using a common source independently—Q.

This completes our discussion of the Synoptic Problem. The fact that Matthew and Luke used Mark and the hypothetical source Q should inform our exegesis. The student can now trace with a high degree of probability the changes made by the two Gospel writers and, with sufficient evidence, posit reasons for these alterations.

Before discussing the basic steps of synoptic exegesis, the student needs to understand the nature of the Synoptics as well as the similarities and dissimilarities between them. This knowledge is best gained by underlining a synopsis and so we now turn to how this may be accomplished.

Underlining a Synopsis

Before outlining the procedure for underlining a synopsis, something needs to be said about the difference between a harmony and a synopsis, though no technical definition divides them. In general, a harmony presents the same event or saying in the life of Jesus from the Gospels in parallel fashion so that the reader can easily harmonize events and sayings. Harmonies are almost always based upon a given chronology of the life of Jesus. Synopses, on the other hand, place parallel accounts of the same event or saying side by side so that the reader can compare similarities and dissimilarities word by word. Thus, whereas a harmony is normally concerned with constructing a life of Jesus by facilitating a broad comparison of *events*, the intention of a synopsis is the careful comparison of *words*.

Before underlining, the student must recognize what a synopsis does and does not do. A synopsis attempts to provide a substantial parallel (there is, of course, a marginal degree of subjectivity in determining what a "substantial parallel" is) to a given saying or pericope by listing the same words alongside that saying or pericope. For example, the synoptic accounts of the death of Jesus may be placed in parallel columns to facilitate ease of comparison (Matt. 27:45–56; Mark 15:33–41; Luke 23:44–49). (At this point, students may want to read this pericope carefully in a synopsis in order to familiarize themselves with the synopsis and the two factors which are immediately obvious: similarity and dissimilarity.

These accounts all mention the presence of darkness from the sixth until the ninth hour largely in the same terms. Only Luke mentions the reason for the sun's darkness (τοῦ ἡλίου ἐκλιπόντος). The fact that the temple veil was torn is reported by both Matthew and Mark at the same point in their narratives (cf. Matt. 27:51; Mark 15:38). Matthew and Mark then report the same facts in largely the same terms (Matt. 27:46–51; Mark 15:34–38). At this point in the narrative Matthew includes two supernatural events which are not found in Mark and Luke, the earthquake and the raising of the dead (Matt. 27:51b–53). All three Synoptics then relate the confession of the centurion. Whereas the introductory elements vary in each Gospel (Matthew: the centurion and others see the magnitude of these supernatural phenomena; Mark: the centurion observes how Jesus died; Luke: the centurion sees what had transpired), the saying itself is in similar terms (Matt. 27:54; Mark 15:39; Luke 23:47). Luke next records something with no parallel in either Matthew or Mark: the response of the crowd (Luke 23:48). Then all three Synoptics record things about the followers of Jesus, though Luke's account is in different terms (Matt. 27:55–56; Mark 15:40–41; Luke 23:49).

Underlining is scientifically objective and neutral in the sense that it does not presuppose a solution to the relationship of the synoptic Gospels. A color in a synopsis merely records an observation. For example, if the word καί in Mark 15:33 and Luke 23:44 is underlined in the same color, this merely indicates that both Mark and Luke have the same term at the same point in the narrative. If Matthew and Mark both use the aorist participle ἀκούσαντες at the same place (Matt. 27:47; Mark 15:35), and it is underlined accordingly, that too simply indicates that Matthew and Mark have used the same word at the same place. It says nothing about their relationship, for such phenomena could be coincidental or interdependent, with the latter susceptible to several explanations.

In underlining, students should work with four colors: blue, yellow (or black for those who have difficulty seeing yellow), red, and green. These colors are recommended by W. R. Farmer *(Synopticon)* and R. H. Stein *(Synoptic Problem).* If the student uses these colors, the underlining may be checked for accuracy using the *Synopticon.*

Following are the rules for underlining:[13]

1. Determine by examination if there is a true parallel by observing whether the sayings and/or events are actually the same. If no true parallel exists, then underlining should not be attempted; the accounts are independent. A good example of this is Matthew 22:1–14 and Luke 14:16–24. Apart from the completely different locations in the Gospels, the two accounts, though largely recording the same story, have almost no words in common and only one time does it extend to two consecutive words (καὶ ἀπέστειλεν in Luke 14:17 and Matt. 22:3).

For a true parallel, the following rules apply:

2. Words that are totally unparalleled (not found in either of the other Gospels) should not be underlined. Naturally, this occurs frequently in narrative sections of the Gospels. A good example can be seen by comparing Matthew 9:14, Mark 2:18, and Luke 5:33 for, though the writers record most of the sayings of Jesus in the same words, the introductions are distinct. (Some students may choose to underline these words as well in another color [e.g., brown].)

3. Words that occur in all three Gospels should be underlined in blue. (This is called the "Triple Tradition.") If the pericope on the

---

13. For help in underlining, see W. R. Farmer, *Synopticon* (Cambridge: Cambridge University Press, 1969); B. de Solages, *A Greek Synopsis of the Gospels: A New Way of Solving the Synoptic Problem* (Leiden: E. J. Brill, 1959). However, possession of these sources must not be seen as a substitute for personal underlining.

death of Jesus discussed earlier is underlined, for example, the following words from Mark 15:33 will be underlined in blue: ὥρας, ἕκτ−, σκότος ἐγένετο ἐφ', τὴν γῆν ἕως ὥρας ἐνάτης.

4. Words that are the same in Matthew and Mark but different in Luke should be underlined in yellow (or black). It is important to note here that one must be sure that Luke does not have the same word(s) for it to be a yellow line. In Matthew 27:46 the following words will be underlined in yellow: ἐνα−, ὥρ−, −εβόησεν ὁ Ἰησοῦς φωνῇ μεγάλῃ, σαβαχθανι, θε−, μου, θε−, μου, με ἐγκατέλιπες. (Note that it is helpful to indicate words which are true, but only partial parallels. In Matthew 27:46, for example, only ἐνα− is underlined in yellow. This shows that though Matthew has the same word [a true parallel], his use of that word is unique— and that part is not underlined.) Others might choose to underline the whole word with a skipped line—indicating "same word, different form" (a partial parallel). However, dual coloring makes both the dissimilarity and similarity immediately visible.

5. Words common to Mark and Luke but not found in Matthew are underlined in green (e.g., in Mark 15:33 and Luke 23:44: καί, ὅλην).

6. Words common to Matthew and Luke but not in Mark are underlined in red. Here is where "objective and neutral" facts become obvious. Most contemporary New Testament scholars accept Markan priority and the existence of a common source between Matthew and Luke (Q). But not everything appearing in red is Q material. Red underlining simply demonstrates a neutral fact: Matthew and Luke, but not Mark, record a given word. This fact is clear in Matthew 27:54 and Luke 23:47, for both authors call the man ὁ ἑκατόνταρχος/−ης; Mark (15:39) calls him ὁ κεντυρίων. The similarity between Matthew and Luke constitutes an objective fact; it does not prove that both Matthew and Luke independently used a hypothetical source. Note that though Matthew and Luke use a different number (Luke singular; Matthew plural) and place the word in a different position, both record the object of the participle ἰδών as the neuter substantival participle of γίνομαι. Further agreements between Matthew and Luke against Mark are found in Mat-

thew 27:55 and Luke 23:49. (It is only when an entire saying is
mostly red that one could conclude that it is from Q.)[14]

This takes care of all possible relationships between Matthew,
Mark, and Luke.[15] Parallels to John are rare and are not of great
concern. (In my synopsis, I have chosen to demonstrate this relationship by highlighting [rather than underlining] the common
words in yellow.)

Underlining a synopsis will prove to be a rewarding, though
tedious, procedure; but once a passage is underlined, it will never
need to be done again. Underlining a synopsis is an eye-opening
exercise which pays great dividends for interpretation. Not long
ago, I visited with a British university professor whose study had
recently been flooded, damaging many papers, books, and reference works. When he commented on the damage, the book he was
most disappointed about losing was Aland's *Synopsis*, "because," he
said, "of all the hours of underlining and making observations in
the columns."

This concludes our discussion of the preliminary issues affecting
synoptic exegesis. We now need to consider the basic steps of
exegeting a pericope.

---

14. An alternate color system may be recommended:
    in place of "non-underlined words," use "red";
    in place of "blue," use "brown";
    in place of "yellow," use "blue";
    in place of "green," use "skipped blue";
    in place of "red," use "green."
The advantage of this coloring system is that each word is underlined and unique
portions become immediately obvious because they are red. Further, the Double
Tradition between Mk–Mt and Mk–Lk is of the same color.

15. Maintaining neutrality in approaching the Synoptic Problem has many
ramifications for exegesis. For example, if one assumes that the synoptic Gospels
are independent, then one will undoubtedly make certain observations that would
not otherwise be made. Similarly, one will avoid other conclusions that would
naturally follow from a different presupposition. More often than not, this "neutral
ground" is little more than the despairing cry of someone who finds the evidence
too complex. But can anyone who is devoted to studying the Bible deliberately
ignore the evidence? For a discussion of the value of source criticism (and underlining), see Stein, *Synoptic Problem*, 139–57.

Part 2

Basic Steps
of Synoptic Exegesis

4

Textual Criticism

In synoptic exegesis, the exegete begins with textual and grammatical analysis, then proceeds to tradition-critical analyses and the analysis of words, investigates motifs and theology, and concludes with an analysis of narrative strategies. These procedures are applied to individual pericopae in order better to ascertain the intention of the author. A statement of this intention is the goal of exegesis; it is then used to satisfy the needs of the individual student (personal edification, preaching, etc.). This chapter concentrates on textual analysis, the foundation for synoptic exegesis. Textual criticism is the science of determining, as far as possible, the original text of the New Testament, and attempting to understand the reasons for changes. (For a more complete presentation of this discipline, see the chapter on textual criticism in the introductory volume to this series.)

Before textual analysis can be undertaken, it is necessary to translate the passage in a rough form (in order to familiarize oneself with the text), identifying every unknown word using Bauer's *Lexicon*. The student needs to recognize that synoptic exegesis does not begin with textual criticism because it is the simplest of steps but because one must know what the text is before one can interpret the text.

Students of the Synoptics should use the twenty-sixth edition of the Nestle-Aland ($=N^{26}$) text rather than the third edition of the United Bible Societies (UBS) text for the following reasons:

1. N^{26} is specifically a student text whereas the UBS text is designed primarily for translators.

2. The apparatus of N[26] is much more complete, containing as many as twenty times the number of variants.
3. The marginalia of N[26] are invaluable and are not found in the UBS text.
4. Standard reference books and commentaries use N[26] (or one of its predecessors) as a foundation text.
5. The Aland *Synopsis* (a superior synopsis) uses the text and apparatus of N[26].

Many have criticized N[26] for being too small, too complex, and failing to provide a translation of the insert. First, though there is a larger edition available from UBS, it is more cumbersome. Second, with practice, the student can, with moderate effort, readily master the essentials of the N[26] apparatus and text. Complexity need not be confused with precision and completeness. Third, UBS does publish an English version of the insert. The only added value of the UBS text is its punctuation apparatus, and many of these discussions are also found in the N[26].

Students should learn how to determine the original text while recognizing that rarely will they find themselves in disagreement with N[26]. There are obviously some passages where certainty can never be reached, but these are rarely significant for interpretation or theology. It is important for students to learn how to read the apparatus of N[26] in order to find interpretative clues for determining the intention of the author. In other words, students need to recognize the significance of the variants (which are probably not original) for interpretation in that many of these function as early commentaries on the text.

A typical example is Matthew 9:9–13. At the end of verse 9, ἠκολούθησεν is changed in some manuscripts to the imperfect (ἠκολούθει), suggesting that Matthew's "following" was a continuous process rather than a simple, one-time event. (The aorist is constative, signifying the fact that Matthew followed Jesus.) In verse 10, a more grammatically trained scribe omits καί, implying that the conjunction should not be included as though two coordinate ideas are being expressed (reclining/presence of sinners). In verse 11, some manuscripts have the second aorist of λέγω rather than the imperfect; this could reflect either a variant of an original Semitic past tense, a substantial difference, or, more probably, the imperfect is used only to add color to the narrative. At any rate, the presence of the aorist cautions the student against reading too much into the imperfect.

The final clause of verse 11 has several variations: (1) one Latin manuscript completely omits ὁ διδάσκαλος ὑμῶν, probably (incorrectly) jumping from one ὁ to the next; (2) another reading harmonizes Matthew with Luke 5:30, where the second person plural is used; and (3) the final reading shows conflation, combining the text's reading with the second variant (the person of the text and the vocabulary of Luke). This illustrates a common feature of the synoptic Gospels—the tendency to harmonize one Gospel with another by conforming the readings. In verse 12, one manuscript adds "Jesus" to avoid any suggestion that someone other than Jesus responded (this, too, is probably harmonization as well). Not only does the addition of αὐτοῖς harmonize Matthew with Mark and Luke, it clarifies those whom Jesus addresses. At the end of verse 13 another harmonization is evident: some manuscripts add εἰς μετάνοιαν, making it clear that Jesus' call had a pointed direction. This example underscores the fact that students need to ask what difference a given variant might have on the meaning of the sentence and pericope.

Textual criticism is a science of probability not certainty. Certain internal principles (not to be confused with rules) have been developed that are now standard procedure for determining which reading is to be preferred. The basic question is which reading best explains the origin of the others. If one can answer this question, one has almost certainly determined the original reading.

There are also external factors. Scholars have detected certain textual resemblances between manuscripts, and have grouped them into text types. The two basic types are Alexandrian and Byzantine; there are two secondary text types, known as Western and Caesarean.[1]

A tendency toward harmonization is characteristic of the synoptic Gospels. In the Synoptics, scribes intentionally altered the texts of the Gospels in order to make them similar. Thus, for example, scribes added the ascription to the shorter form of the Lord's Prayer in Luke 11:4 to conform Luke's account to Matthew's (Matt. 6:9–13). In addition to this harmonization tendency, a particular solution to

---

1. For the classification of manuscripts by types, see J. H. Greenlee, *An Introduction to New Testament Textual Criticism* (Grand Rapids: Eerdmans, 1974), 117–18.

the Synoptic Problem should affect one's text-critical decisions. If one accepts Markan priority, such a solution will need to be considered as one examines textual matters.[2]

Textual criticism is especially important for those who maintain a high view of Scripture. After roughly translating the text, determining the original text, and using the apparatus to obtain information on what scribes were doing to the text, grammatical analysis should commence.

---

2. Taking Matthew 9:9–13 as an example, the reading αὐτοῖς in verse 12 may be given more consideration since it is found in Mark, and Mark is considered by many to have been the source of Matthew.

5

Grammatical Analysis

O nce a preliminary translation has been rendered and the text has been established, the exegete can begin analyzing the grammatical and syntactical relations of the words, clauses, and sentences in a given pericope. Fortunately for the novice exegete, the grammar and syntax of the Synoptics, except for an occasional classical flourish in Luke, are not difficult, making the Synoptics a good place to begin grammatical exegesis.

Grammar and syntax constitute the essence of exegesis. The student of the Synoptics needs to recognize that, until the principles of grammar and syntax are mastered so that most passages in Matthew, Mark, and Luke can be diagrammed, the exegetical task will be hindered.

The purpose of diagramming is to identify the grammatical function of every word in a particular sentence. If the proper grammatical location cannot be demonstrated by means of a diagram, it is unlikely that the grammatical function of the given word is known. And exegesis cannot proceed to syntax if grammar is not comprehended.

Synoptic Grammar

Before presenting an example of diagramming and commenting on grammatical analysis, a few observations about synoptic grammar and syntax must be made. It is not possible to give a comprehensive description of the style of each of the Synoptics; instead, some general observations will be offered.

It is generally agreed that the major reason for the unique features of synoptic Greek is the influence of Semitic patterns upon Greek grammar. The exegete who is familiar with both Greek and Hebrew will undoubtedly appreciate more fully the nature of synoptic Greek.[1] But it should not be supposed that each of the Evangelists has the same style. Whereas Mark's and Matthew's style are common, Luke has a much more sophisticated manner. Moreover, probably due to sources and traditions, even an individual author's style can vary from passage to passage.

In general the Synoptics, expecially Matthew and Mark, have a proclivity for coordination rather than subordination of clauses, a grammatical feature known as parataxis. Instead of treating an introductory clause in a subordinate fashion, the synoptic authors often join two sentences with καί (cf. Mark 6:14; 15:25; Matt. 18:21). Mark's Gospel in particular is characterized by redundancy, the seemingly needless repetition of words and expressions (e.g., 1:28; 4:2; 6:25; 13:19). The wise interpreter will observe this as a feature of repetition, not logical distinction. Another characteristic feature of the Synoptics, largely because of the abundance of narrative, is the frequent use of the so-called historic present—"historic" because it is something which actually took place in the past but is being depicted as occurring in the present. Mark has approximately 150 uses, Matthew approximately 90, and Luke only 9 (e.g., Matt. 8:7; 17:25; 19:20).

The Gospel authors not only favor parataxis; they also regularly avoid the use of conjunctions (asyndeton, a sentence without grammatical connection; see e.g., Matt. 4:7; 27:65; Mark 14:42; Luke 6:27–28). Probably due to Semitic influence, there is an abundance

---

1. A brief survey of the style of each of the synoptic writers can be found in N. Turner, "Style," in *A Grammar of New Testament Greek*, ed. by J. H. Moulton, W. F. Howard, and N. Turner, 4:11–63 (Edinburgh: T. & T. Clark, 1976). A helpful discussion of Semitisms in the New Testament can be found in C. F. D. Moule, *An Idiom Book of New Testament Greek*, 2d ed. (Cambridge: Cambridge University Press, 1963), 171–91; R. A. Martin, *Syntactical Evidence of Semitic Sources in Greek Documents* (Missoula, Mont.: Scholar's Press, 1974); R. A. Martin, *Syntax Criticism of the Synoptic Gospels* (Lewiston, N.Y.: Edwin Mellen, 1987).

of pleonastic participles in the Synoptics (participles which are not grammatically necessary and tend to be redundant). The most noticeable example is the use of ἀποκριθείς with a verb of speaking (Matt. 8:8; other examples include Matt. 9:18; 21:35; Luke 15:18). Again, because the Gospels are mostly narrative in nature, there are many examples of the genitive absolute. Such introductions often begin a pericope (e.g., Matt. 8:1, 5; Mark 1:32; Luke 4:40).

Exemplar: Matthew 6:1–4

Overview of Matthew 6:1–18

In Matthew 6:1–18, verse 1 functions as the thematic statement of the entire pericope. In spite of an apparent digression in verses 7–15 (indicated by a different structural pattern), the central thrust of the passage is clearly not doing righteous acts in order to gain the glory of men. This theme is explicated (note the inferential οὖν in v. 2) using three specific examples: almsgiving (vv. 2–4), prayer (vv. 5–15), and fasting (vv. 16–18).

The three illustrations are structurally similar,[2] as can be discovered by underlining. Each begins with an indefinite temporal clause (ὅταν [vv. 2, 5, 16]), which is followed by a prohibition (μὴ σαλπίσῃς; οὐκ ἔσεσθε; μὴ γίνεσθε). This, in turn, is followed by a comparative clause (ὥσπερ; ὡς) and a resultative clause (ὅπως). Jesus then offers a revelatory condemnation (ἀμὴν λέγω ὑμιν,

---

2. It needs to be reiterated here that 6:7–15, though fitting thematically with 6:5–6 (prayer), clashes with the thematic statement (hypocritical religious behavior) since 6:7–15 is concerned, not with hypocrites', but with Gentiles' abuse of prayer. Furthermore, the pattern is different: (1) Matthew 6:7–15 begins, not with an indefinite temporal clause, but with a participle; (2) Gentiles, not Jewish hypocrites, are in view; (3) there is no revelatory comment; (4) there is not a similarly phrased promise; and (5) the Lord's Prayer is a lengthy illustration of the simple (in contrast to verbose) prayer Jesus expects. Further, there is a parallel to Matthew 6:14–15 in a completely different context in Mark 11:25–26. The Lukan parallel to the Lord's Prayer is also in a different context (Luke 11:2–4). I would suggest that Matthew (or a previous Christian teacher) has thematically combined two teachings on prayer for reasons other than strict chronology, augmenting 6:5–6 with 6:7–13(14–15). This observation on parallels is confirmed by the structural dissimilarity of 6:1–6, 16–18, and 6:7–15.

ἀπέχουσιν τὸν μισθὸν αὐτῶν) and, using an adversative and an emphatic personal pronoun (σοῦ δὲ ποιοῦντος; σὺ δὲ ὅταν προσεύχῃ; σὺ δὲ νηστεύων [vv. 3, 6, 17]) explains to the disciples how they are to perform these religious deeds righteously (μὴ γνώτω . . . ; εἴσελθε . . . ; ἄλειψαί . . .). The conclusion, also stated in verse 1, is that their Father, "who is in the heavens," will reward them. This pattern becomes clear when the passage is carefully diagrammed. In broad outline, then, there are four features:

1. An indefinite temporal clause, detailing a certain kind of religious deed
2, Jesus' prohibition of hypocritical behavior
3. His revelatory condemnation
4. His contrasting behavioral direction along with the promise of reward for proper performance

Diagram of Matthew 6:1–4

The following example (table 4) illustrates the technique and potential value of diagramming in the Synoptics.

Grammatical Analysis of Matthew 6:1–4

Since the subject of the verb in 6:1 is unexpressed, it is constructed and placed within brackets ([ὑμεῖς]). The objective infinitive (μὴ ποιεῖν) is placed as the object of the verb. That infinitive, in turn, has an object (τὴν δικαιοσύνην). The adverbial phrase ἔμπροσθεν τῶν ἀνθρώπων is subordinate to the main verbal construction of 6:1 (προσέχετε μὴ ποιεῖν), as is the infinitive phrase of purpose (πρὸς τὸ θεαθῆναι αὐτοῖς). The dative (αὐτοῖς), as a dative of agency, can be placed after the infinitive (as shown) or subordinate to that infinitive, expressing an adverbial relation.

The second part of 6:1 is a conditional sentence. The protasis is placed first; a solidus and an arrow point to its logical fulfillment in the apodosis. The bracketed words of the protasis ([ὑμεῖς προσέχετε μὴ . . .]) are assumed. The apodosis demands a reconstructed subject ([ὑμεῖς]) and is a simple construction (subject-verb-direct object). The prepositional phrase (παρὰ τῷ πατρί) is proba-

Table 4

Diagram of Matthew 6:1–4

6:1 δὲ [ὑμεῖς] προσέχετε μὴ ποιεῖν τὴν δικαιοσύνην
                     ὑμῶν
                     ἔμπροσθεν τῶν ἀνθρώπων
                     πρὸς τὸ θεαθῆναι αὐτοῖς
  δὲ εἰ μὴ [ὑμεῖς προσέχετε μὴ . . .]
  γε → [ὑμεῖς] οὐκ ἔχετε μισθὸν
                 παρὰ τῷ πατρὶ
                     ὑμῶν
                     τῷ [ἐστιν] ἐν τοῖς οὐρανοῖς
6:2 οὖν [σὺ] μὴ σαλπίσῃς
             ἔμπροσθέν σου
             ὅταν [σὺ] ποιῇς ἐλεημοσύνην
             ὥσπερ οἱ ὑποκριταὶ ποιοῦσιν
                     ἐν ταῖς ῥύμαις
                     ὅπως [αὐτοὶ] δοξασθῶσιν
                           ὑπὸ τ. ἀνθρ.
  [ἐγὼ] λέγω [ὅτι] ὑμῖν
      ἀμὴν
        [αὐτοὶ] ἀπέχουσιν τὸν μισθὸν
                     αὐτῶν
6:3 δὲ σοῦ ποιοῦντος ἐλεημοσύνην
    ἡ ἀριστερά μὴ γνώτω (τί ἡ δεξιά ποιεῖ)
    σου   σου
6:4   ὅπως ἡ ἐλεημοσύνη ᾖ ἐν τῷ κρυπτῷ
                  σου
  καὶ ὁ πατήρ ἀποδώσει σοι
  σου
  ὁ βλέπων
    ἐν τῷ κρυπτῷ

bly adverbial and, therefore, subordinate to the verb. After a simple personal pronoun, an article functioning as a relative pronoun introduces a relative clause (τῷ [ἐστιν] ἐν τοῖς οὐρανοῖς).

Only a few pertinent observations will be made for 6:2–4. Three adverbial subordinate clauses in 6:2 modify the prohibition, with two additional adverbial modifications of ποιοῦσιν in the ὥσπερ clause. The omitted conjunction ὅτι has been reconstructed; the direct quotation is then placed immediately under the implied object ([ὅτι]) of the verb of speaking and is diagrammed as a sentence.

The genitive absolute of 6:3 is rearranged in order to show how it functions at a deep structure level (as subject and verb). The adversative particle (δὲ) introduces a contrast to the previous sentence: instead of performing alms as the hypocrites do, the disciples are to do so without self-conscious congratulation. The object of the verb (γνώτω) is the entire τί clause. (Because the object in this case is more than one word, I have enclosed the entire object in parentheses.)

The last verse (6:4) begins with an adverbial clause (ὅπως) which modifies the verb of 6:3 (γνώτω); this clause forms a copulative sentence, the predicate expressing what "might be done in secret." Following καί is a simple sentence consisting of a subject, verb, and indirect object; the object is probably [μισθόν]. The subject of this sentence (ὁ πατήρ) is modified by a personal pronoun (σου) and an adjectival participial phrase (ὁ βλέπων); the latter is modified, in turn, by an adverbial prepositional phrase (ἐν τῷ κρυπτῷ).

After completing a grammatical analysis of the passage, the student should carefully examine syntax, asking questions such as why the author chooses the present tense (ἔχετε) in the apodosis of 6:1 and in 6:2 (ἀπέχουσιν), and what significance the choice of an aorist prohibitory subjunctive in 6:2 has.

Following a thorough analysis of syntax, the student should consult the appendices and appropriate sections of the major grammars, and only then various commentaries for grammar and syntax. Further background study may be needed, and the student's original translation can be revised as necessary.

In the next three chapters, we shall examine the methods most commonly used in synoptic studies, looking at the tradition-critical process (history, form criticism, redaction criticism).

6

Tradition Analysis
Historical Criticism

In chapter 1 we discussed the three-dimensional nature of the Gospels. Each passage in the Gospels records an event or saying which purports to come from the life of Jesus which was first transmitted by the early church in oral and written forms and only later written down in its present canonical shape. The discipline concerned with tracing this development is known as tradition criticism. This chapter is concerned with the first of these stages, with "what happened."

In light of contemporary discussions regarding faith and history, it is important to ask questions about the factual reliability of the Gospels and to learn the proper method for examining their historicity.[1] However, the goal of this process is not simply to determine what did or did not happen, however useful that determination might be to historians; instead, the goal is to inquire if such a process sheds light on the Gospels themselves.

Before analyzing this method, the term *authentic* needs clarification. Though some scholars have argued that anything which is historically significant is "authentic" (e.g., Jesus was not physically

---

1. A helpful book documenting the historical reliability of the Gospels is C. L. Blomberg, *The Historical Reliability of the Gospels* (Downers Grove: Inter-Varsity, 1987). See also J. D. G. Dunn, *The Evidence for Jesus: The Impact of Scholarship on Our Understanding of How Christianity Began* (Philadelphia: Westminster, 1985), esp. 1–28.

raised from the dead but such an idea is significant for the Christian's life), they are only clouding the water. Accordingly, most scholars use the term *authentic* to refer to any datum which coheres and corresponds adequately with what Jesus said or did. These elements of correspondence and coherence are vital for understanding the nature of the Gospels; only rarely do we have verbatim (known among scholars as the *ipsissima verba*) reports of Jesus' sayings, the rare exceptions being Aramaic utterances (e.g., Mark 5:41: *talitha cum*). A good example of correspondence and coherence, as compared with verbatim report, can be found in Matthew 10:32 and Luke 12:8. (The line diagram below facilitates comparison.)

Luke 12:8: πᾶς ὃς ἂν ὁμολογήσῃ ἐν ἐμοὶ ἔμπροσθεν τῶν ἀνθρώπων

Matthew 10:32: πᾶς ὅστις ὁμολογήσει ἐν ἐμοὶ ἔμπροσθεν τῶν ἀνθρώπων

Luke: καὶ ὁ υἱὸς τοῦ ἀνθρώπου ὁμολογήσει ἐν αὐτῷ ἔμπροσθεν . . .

Matthew: κἀγὼ   ὁμολογήσω ἐν αὐτῷ ἔμπροσθεν . . .

The question of historicity concerns the terms ὁ υἱὸς τοῦ ἀνθρώπου and ἐγώ (in our text κἀγώ). Which of these did Jesus say? Did he say "Son of man" or did he say "I"? At one level, obviously, there is a formal contradiction between the two; but since the Gospels are a depiction of what Jesus said and since "Son of man" can be otherwise adequately rendered as "I," there is a high degree of correspondence to, and coherence with, what Jesus intended in this saying. Both depictions are, therefore, "authentic."

Definition and Analysis

Tradition criticism may be defined as a discipline of historians designed to uncover authentic data about Jesus of Nazareth, as distinguished from data which the early church added to the traditions, by utilizing various criteria. Several considerations follow from this definition.

First, the primary goal of tradition criticism is to separate what is authentic from what is inauthentic. Second, the discipline must assume that individual sayings and other data in the Gospels have been added to the traditions and have no historical anchor in the life of Jesus. A sceptical, but not uncommon, example of this is Perrin's classic introductory statement:

> The early Church made no attempt to distinguish between the words the earthly Jesus had spoken and those spoken by the risen Lord through a prophet in the community, nor between the original teaching of Jesus and the new understanding and reformulation of that teaching reached in the catechesis or parenesis of the Church under the guidance of the Lord of the Church. The early Church absolutely and completely identified the risen Lord of her experience with the earthly Jesus of Nazareth and created for her purposes, which she conceived to be his, the literary form of the Gospel, in which words and deeds ascribed in her consciousness to both the earthly Jesus and the risen Lord were set down in terms of the former.[2]

In agreement with Perrin, many scholars today argue that the burden of proof is upon those who argue *for* authenticity.[3]

A final observation is that tradition critics assume that various criteria can be used to separate what is authentic from what is inauthentic. Though different scholars have utilized various criteria, all accept the validity of those criteria. In fact, most would argue that these are the "tools of the historian's trade." What, then, are these criteria?

The Criteria of Authenticity

Scholars have developed six standard criteria which are used to evaluate the authenticity of the Gospel accounts; however, the crite-

---

2. N. Perrin, *Rediscovering the Teaching of Jesus* (New York: Harper & Row, 1967), 15.

3. Ibid., 39.

ria vary in weight from scholar to scholar.[4] Our purpose is to define the various criteria in use.

The first criterion is *dissimilarity*: "The earliest form of a saying we can reach may be regarded as authentic if it can be shown to be dissimilar to characteristic emphases both of ancient Judaism and of the early Church, and this will particularly be the case where Christian tradition oriented towards Judaism can be shown to have modified the saying away from its original emphasis."[5] This criterion applies to what is dissimilar both to Judaism and to Christianity, not just to one or the other, as well as to characteristic emphases. This criterion has been used, for example, to demonstrate the authenticity of Jesus' teaching on the presence of the kingdom when no such emphasis had occurred in Judaism.

The second criterion is *coherence*: "Material from the earliest strata of the tradition may be accepted as authentic if it can be shown to cohere with material established as authentic by means of the criterion of dissimilarity."[6] This criterion is used: (1) with material which *cannot* be authenticated with the criterion of dissimilarity; and (2) with material which is *substantially compatible* with the material established as authentic by the criterion of dissimilarity. (How one is able to detect the difference is not defined.) For example, if one omits Luke 16:8–9 from the parable of the unjust steward (vv. 1–9) because it is inauthentic, one has a parable concerned with the eschatological crisis effected by Jesus and the necessity of deciding for him now. This is coherent with Jesus' teaching on the presence of the kingdom.[7]

The third standard criterion is *multiple attestation*—"This is a proposal to accept as authentic material which is attested in all, or

---

4. The literature on the criteria is voluminous. The following works are fundamental: R. S. Barbour, *Traditio-Historical Criticism of the Gospels: Some Comments on Current Methods* (London: SPCK, 1972); D. L. Mealand, "The Dissimilarity Test," *Scottish Journal of Theology* 31 (1978): 41–50; M. D. Hooker, "Christology and Methodology," *New Testament Studies* 17 (1970–1971): 480–87; R. N. Longenecker, "Literary Criteria in Life of Jesus Research: An Evaluation and Proposal," in *Current Issues in Biblical and Patristic Interpretation*, ed. by G. F. Hawthorne, 217–29 (Grand Rapids: Eerdmans, 1975); G. R. Osborne, "The Evangelical and *Traditionsgeschichte*," *Journal of the Evangelical Theological Society* 21 (1978): 117–30; B. F. Meyer, *The Aims of Jesus* (London: SCM, 1979), 76–94.

5. Perrin, *Rediscovering*, 39.

6. Ibid., 43.

7. Ibid., 114–15.

most, of the sources which can be discerned behind the Synoptic Gospels"[8] (these sources are Q, Mk, M, and L). This criterion is used to establish motifs, not individual sayings or deeds of Jesus.[9] It is also useful when the motif is found in more than one form (e.g., I-sayings, pronouncement stories, etc.; see chap. 7). This criterion should be used *only after* the more specific criteria of dissimilarity and coherence have been used. For example, Jesus practiced table fellowship with, and forgiveness of, sinners (cf. Mark 2:15:17; Q: Matt. 11:18–19; L: Luke 15:1–2; M: Matt. 21:28–32); and this practice is found in pronouncements, dominical sayings, and parables.

A fourth criterion is that of *Semitisms:* "Since it seems certain that the mother tongue of Jesus was Aramaic, and in particular a Galilean dialect of Aramaic, the presence of Aramaic linguistic characteristics in our Greek Gospel materials argues in favor of the primitiveness of those particular traditions and the more primitive a tradition is, the more likely it is that it stems from Jesus."[10] An obvious example is Mark 15:34.[11]

The fifth criterion is that of *divergent traditions.* D. G. A. Calvert, among others, argues that when an author preserves traditions which do not "especially serve his purpose [they] may well be taken as testimony to the authenticity of that material."[12] Others find this criterion useful in finding competing traditions between Gospels or within a Gospel. That is, when two authors preserve a tradition but one has modified it to some degree (cf. Mark 10:11–12 with Matt. 5:32; 19:9) or when one author has a tradition which "competes" with another (Matt. 10:5–6 and 28:16–20), we may utilize this criterion.

The final criterion is *primitive eschatology.* Bultmann and his followers used the eschatological content of a given logion as a test for all the sayings of Jesus. In other words, if it evinces imminency

---

8. Ibid., 45.

9. Ibid., 46–47.

10. R. H. Stein, "The 'Criteria' for Authenticity," *Gospel Perspectives* (Sheffield: JSOT, 1980), 1:233–34.

11. For further clarification of this criterion, see J. Jeremias, *New Testament Theology: The Proclamation of Jesus* (New York: Scribners, 1971), esp. 1–37.

12. D. G. A. Calvert, "An Examination of the Criteria for Distinguishing the Authentic Words of Jesus," *New Testament Studies* 18 (1972): 219.

(= primitive eschatology), it is from Jesus.[13] This criterion would authenticate such verses as Mark 9:1 and 13:30.

At one level these criteria (apart from the last in that it is concerned with a feature of the teaching of Jesus established as authentic on other grounds) are legitimate methods for determining what is reasonably historical.

Having presented the various criteria utilized in the discussion of the historical Jesus, we now need to evaluate their usefulness for synoptic exegesis.

Positive Evaluation of the Criteria of Authenticity

One of the positive results of this methodological clarification has been that scholars are required to verify their conclusions on the basis of a controllable and reasonably objective method. The scientific method is essentially that of question, hypothesis, and verification. Thus, the historian first asks whether Jesus was in fact raised from the dead. Then he or she seeks to construct a hypothesis: Jesus was in fact raised from the dead. Finally, he or she seeks to verify or deny that hypothesis by examining all the data. Methodological rigor is made possible by the use of criteria.

Furthermore, these criteria point to the probabilistic nature of all historical research. When any scholar demands of someone that he prove X happened with absolute certainty, he is asking for more than any historian can demonstrate.

The greatest value of the criteria is that they put the Gospels on an open table for all to discuss and evaluate with mutually acceptable tools. Such a procedure, if followed honestly, should lead to conclusions which are confirmed by other historians using the same methods.

Negative Evaluation of the Criteria of Authenticity

First, one recognizes immediately the importance and role of presuppositions in Gospel studies. G. Vermes notes:

---

13. See R. Bultmann, *Theology of the New Testament* (New York: Scribners, 1951), 1:4–11.

Most people, whether they admit it or not, approach the Gospels with preconceived ideas. Christians read them in the light of their faith; Jews, primed with age-old suspicion; agnostics, ready to be scandalized; and professional New Testament experts, wearing the blinkers of their trade. Yet it should not be beyond the capabilities of an educated man to sit down and with *an open mind empty of prejudice* read the accounts of Mark, Matthew and Luke as though for the first time.[14]

Vermes contends that "in another [respect], it [his search for Jesus] is unusual: that it has been made without—*so far as I am consciously aware*—*any ulterior motive*," and goes on to speak of "the inalienable right of the historian to pursue a course *independent of beliefs*."[15] Now we must applaud any effort to "bracket off" personal beliefs and presuppositions in order to discover the truth more clearly; but, in fact, one cannot completely discard one's presuppositions and thereby attain complete objectivity.[16]

A second problem with the criteria is the decisive role of the so-called burden of proof. When two reputable scholars can come to diametrically opposed conclusions regarding burden of proof, then one needs to recognize its significance (and probably their own presuppositions as well). Perrin argues that *"the nature of the Synoptic tradition is such that the burden of proof will be upon the claim to authenticity,"*[17] while Jeremias states that "in the Synoptic tradition it is the inauthenticity, and not the authenticity, of the sayings of Jesus that must be demonstrated."[18]

---

14. G. Vermes, *Jesus the Jew: An Historian's Reading of the Gospels* (Philadelphia: Fortress, 1973), 19; emphasis added.

15. G. Vermes, *Jesus and the World of Judaism* (Philadelphia: Fortress, 1983), 1, 2, respectively; emphasis added.

16. G. N. Stanton has written a helpful essay on presuppositions in New Testament exegesis; see "Presuppositions in New Testament Criticism," in *New Testament Interpretation: Essays on Principles and Methods,* ed. by I. H. Marshall, 60–71 (Grand Rapids: Eerdmans, 1977). Stanton argues that three safeguards will help avoid interpreting in a way which merely seeks to confirm one's prejudices and presuppositions: (1) awareness of one's presuppositions; (2) the historical-critical method (it checks unbridled subjectivism); (3) the interpreter's intentional willingness to let his own presuppositions be challenged and modified by the texts themselves. One cannot emphasize the latter safeguard enough.

17. Perrin, *Rediscovering,* 39.

18. Jeremias, *New Testament Theology,* 37.

This issue of the burden of proof cannot be minimized. One's stance in this regard is absolutely crucial in doing history, and it must not be thought that a neutral stance is in fact neutral. There are factors which tip the burden of proof in favor of "authentic until proven otherwise." Stein, for instance, has argued that there are enough factors favoring reliability that one should begin by assuming authenticity. These include: (1) the presence of eyewitnesses (if not when the Gospels themselves were written, at least for the oral stages); (2) the concern of leaders in Jerusalem for preservation; (3) the high view of traditions (Rom. 6:17; 1 Cor. 7:10, 12); (4) the faithfulness of the early church in preserving difficult sayings of Jesus (Matt. 10:5–6; Mark 9:1; 13:32); (5) the Gospels' omission of burning issues concerning the early church; and (6) the ancient's ability to remember.[19]

These factors demonstrate convincingly that one's orientation should be in favor of authenticity. The burden of proof, then, is upon those who deny authenticity. However, anyone who takes a position regarding the authenticity of any given datum in the Gospels should be able to offer reasonable arguments for that view— and quite apart from a simple statement of presuppositions.

A third problem with the criteria concerns their basic orientation. In light of the burden of proof, even the terms used should be adjusted to fit the task of the historian and the nature of the evidence. Thus, if the burden of proof is upon the one who denies authenticity, then the criteria must be named and defined accordingly. Consequently, if the preceding argument is cogent, the criteria should more accurately be called *indices of authenticity*. To use the term *criteria* is to prejudge the data since the data are then being asked to meet the criteria. But, it is not the data which are being called into judgment when the burden of proof favors authenticity; instead, the scholar who denies such is on trial. Thus, each criterion (index) is to be used positively. If a given datum fits an index, it is to be considered genuine or authentic.

Fourth, another problem of the criteria is the inherent limitation of methods. No method can ever be assumed to be absolutely

---

19. Stein, "'Criteria,'" 225–63, esp. 225–28. For a philosophical perspective, see S. C. Goetz and C. L. Blomberg, "The Burden of Proof," *Journal for the Study of the New Testament* 11 (1981): 39–63.

final and inerrant; rather, every method is in need of constant adjustment as experience is gained and knowledge is acquired. This will mean that there may be a difference between what is "authentic" and what is "proven to be authentic," between what is "inauthentic" and what is "proven to be inauthentic" (i.e., between what a method can and cannot do). Just because a method cannot prove a report to be authentic does not mean that this report does not in fact correspond to, or cohere with, what happened. All of this leads to the following proposition: What is inauthentic can only be judged as such by demonstrating that X could not have happened as described.

Fifth, there are serious problems in what may be called the principle of elimination—a standard procedure in tradition criticism which eliminates what is judged to be inauthentic from the pool of evidence in order to clear the way for a historically responsible account of what Jesus was really like. However, this procedure assumes too narrow a definition of "authentic." A more nuanced view will lead to different conclusions; for something to be judged inauthentic means that someone must argue that a given account does not or cannot correspond to what Jesus said or did. The evidence itself points us to a more flexible use of the term *authentic*.

In the Synoptics we are dealing with translated and abbreviated sayings of, and facts about, Jesus. Now it is a fact that all translation and abbreviation means, to one degree or another, interpretation. Thus, if we judge something to be inauthentic, we must argue that the depiction of Jesus does not correspond to the reality or that the interpretation of that event or saying does not correspond to what was done or said. In other words, we might argue that X was not, in fact, said by Jesus in the precise form in which we now have it; but it still is not a misrepresentation of what he said and is therefore authentic. For example, did Jesus originally say "I" or "Son of Man" in the Q logion now found in Matthew 10:32 (cf. Luke 12:8)? Let us suppose that Jesus said "Son of Man." This means that on one level Matthew 10:32 ("I") is inauthentic and therefore to be discarded as evidence for Jesus' self-consciousness. However, since "I" does not misrepresent what Jesus said, then it can be judged to be authentic though not actually said by him.

In conclusion, it is questionable whether scholars are entitled to discard information from the Gospels as inauthentic so casually. In order to do so, scholars must demonstrate that a given report misrepresents what Jesus said or did—and the Gospel texts stand up quite securely against such a procedure. This "principle of elimination," then, demands more careful attention.

A final argument which can be lodged against the criteria concerns how one is to read literature, in particular, religious literature. In recent years scholars of all confessions and presuppositions have grown weary of the dead-end usage of the historical-critical method because it leads to results which are not coherent with the data. Surprisingly, one of the centers of this dissatisfaction has been Tübingen University in Germany. Scholars are now arguing that for genuine understanding to take place, the interpreter must sympathize with the views espoused in the texts themselves. Otherwise, one's orientation will distort the interpretation.[20]

The criteria (indices) have some important limitations. Yet they are of value since they are the best tools New Testament historians have for determining what is authentic. Though they do have problems, the indices can be used so thoroughly in most cases that the historian can close a synopsis with a reasonable conclusion.

Indices Useful for Exegesis

First, one should take seriously the attribution of a given saying to Jesus (index of attribution of a saying). If a given saying is at-

---

20. One example of the concern with developing a hermeneutic that corresponds to the texts themselves can be seen in P. Stuhlmacher, *Vom Verstehen des Neuen Testaments*, NTD Ergänzungsreihe 6 (Göttingen: Vandenhoeck & Ruprecht, 1979), and *Historical Criticism and Theological Interpretation of Scripture* (Philadelphia: Fortress, 1977). Stuhlmacher states:

> The principle of inspiration points up in hermeneutical fashion that the scripture as witness to the revelation possesses an independent power and efficacy which cannot be overtaken or levelled by the most intense pursuit of a systematic exegesis, that scripture cannot be understood in isolation from the referent and experience of the church and lived faith, and *that theological interpretation can be carried on only within the horizon of a concept of truth which allows the historical contact or encounter of immanence with transcendence.* (*Historical Criticism*, 60; emphasis added)

See also F. Hahn, *Historical Investigation and New Testament Faith: Two Lectures* (Philadelphia: Fortress, 1983); R. G. Gruenler, *New Approaches to Jesus and the Gospels* (Grand Rapids: Baker, 1982).

tributed to Jesus, strong evidence must be offered in order to convince the exegete that it was actually uttered by someone else and many reject the hypothesis that early Christian prophets uttered words in the name of Jesus.[21]

Second, a given datum is authentic if it is dissimilar to characteristic emphases both in Judaism and Christianity (index of dissimilarity). This index is hazardous but still useful. It is problematic in that one must assume that there was no continuity between Judaism and Jesus as well as between Jesus and the early church—and this is impossible. Furthermore, all this index can give us is what is unique to Jesus, not necessarily what is characteristic of him (and the latter is more often what is needed). This index also assumes greater historical awareness of Judaism at the time of Jesus and the early church than is possible with the present state of our knowledge. Despite the above problems, if a given datum does fit this index, it unquestionably comes from Jesus and can be used confidently to construct a portrait of Jesus.

Third, a given datum is authentic if it is found in more than one of the Gospel sources (index of multiple sources). (These sources are M, Mark, Q, and L.) The same index applies to sayings or events which occur in different forms (see chap. 7). But again there are problems. For instance, not only does this index usually require a solution to the Synoptic Problem, it also does not allow for the authenticity of a given saying/event if that datum occurs in only one source (e.g., Luke 15:11–32). In this regard, C. F. D. Moule has aptly remarked: "I see no reason to reject a tradition merely because it appears in only one stream, provided it is not intrinsically improbable or contradicted by the other."[22] And so again, though this index has limitations, it may at times prove useful.

---

21. See J. D. G. Dunn, "Prophetic 'I'-Sayings and the Jesus Traditions," *New Testament Studies* 24 (1978): 175–98; D. Hill, *New Testament Prophecy* (Atlanta: John Knox, 1979), 160–85; D. E. Aune, *Prophecy in Early Christianity and the Ancient Mediterranean World* (Grand Rapids: Eerdmans, 1983), 233–45; but cf. now G. F. Hawthorne, "The Role of the Christian Prophets in the Gospel Tradition," in *Tradition and Interpretation in the New Testament: Essays in Honor of E. Earle Ellis for His 60th Birthday*, 119–33 (Grand Rapids: Eerdmans, 1987).

22. C. F. D. Moule, *The Phenomenon of the New Testament* (London: SCM, 1967), 71.

Fourth, a given datum is authentic if it diverges from characteristic theological patterns in the early church (index of divergency of thought patterns).[23] As with the other indices, this one also has its problems. Without proper caution, it can assume greater knowledge of the early church than is possible; it also tends to distinguish the New Testament writers more than necessary. Nevertheless, no one doubts that this index establishes the authenticity of difficult sayings like Mark 13:32; but one must ask if the supposed divergence is not more a matter of our inability than an actual "divergence of thought."

Fifth, a given datum is authentic if it is an obvious translation or reflection of a Semitic origin (index of Semitic milieu). But this index is not foolproof since, if the early Christians invented data about Jesus and were also Aramaic-speaking, we would expect their inventions to reflect a Semitic milieu. Conversely, the index is limited because a good translator can make an idiom in one language (Hebrew/Aramaic) carry over into another (Greek). Furthermore, it is not stretching the facts to argue that Jesus knew some Greek.[24]

Finally, a given datum which does not fit with the above indices, but is coherent with and does not add appreciable information to those data which do fit, is authentic (index of coherency). Yet how does one decide what is coherent? There is actually little value in this index simply because it is so slippery. If one wants to use this index broadly (as it ought to be), then it seems nothing in the Gospel traditions would be blatantly incoherent.

Value of the Indices

These then are the standard critical indices applied to the Gospels in order to determine authenticity. When used positively, the indices point undeniably toward the essential reliability of the synoptic Gospels. Yet is there any value in discerning what is authentic from what is inauthentic?

---

23. See D. G. A. Calvert, "An Examination of the Criteria for Distinguishing the Authentic Words of Jesus," *New Testament Studies* 18 (1972): 570–81.

24. See Jeremias, *New Testament Theology*, 29–37; Jeremias, *The Prayers of Jesus* (London: SCM, 1967), 108–15; J. N. Sevenster, *Do You Know Greek?* (Leiden: E. J. Brill, 1968).

The answer to this question is "Yes." At the end of chapter 8 more attention will be given to answering this question. A few comments are, however, in order here. Though many scholars today contend that, while whether or not something recorded in Mark happened makes a difference for constructing history from Mark, it makes no difference whatsoever for interpreting Mark. There is a serious problem with this view, namely, it assumes that Mark's intention is absent of referentiality (i.e., that Mark is not referring to something outside the text as he writes). Few are convinced today that the Gospel writers are never referring to extra-textual factors when they write. And if Mark is intentionally referring to an event in the life of Jesus, then he is misleading his readers if his reference is bogus (see the appendix).

What value, then, does tradition criticism, as a system of verification, have for interpretation? Admittedly, the primary value is apologetical and historical. Through the use of these criteria, scholars can demonstrate facts about Jesus which become pathways on which to journey in the quest for the historical Jesus, a quest with a goal that has proved illuminating throughout the course of history. And, if God revealed himself in Jesus of Nazareth, in the actions and sayings of Jesus, then knowledge of those events is significant. The criteria have also greatly aided scholars in the determination of the nature of the Gospel genre. By demonstrating that events and sayings are authentic, it becomes clear to scholars that the Gospel writers are writing referentially and are referentially constrained— and if they are writing in such a manner, then this helps us to define just what a Gospel is. Finally, in discovering information about Jesus through these criteria, one is led to investigate the other factors in the background of Jesus in order to clarify the event and possibly the text.

This rather lengthy discussion about tradition criticism has led us back to Jesus and the earliest layer of our Gospels. Form criticism has been developed to ascertain what took place from the time of Jesus to the written sources. It is to a consideration of this discipline that we now turn.

7

Tradition Analysis
Form Criticism

Following the determination of the reliability of a given event or saying, tradition analysis next seeks to discern how that tradition was transmitted orally by the early church and to discover the type of setting which fostered that transmission. The discipline concerned with delineating the supposed "forms" in which a tradition was transmitted is called form criticism. It is the purpose of this chapter to define, explain, and evaluate the usefulness of form criticism for synoptic exegesis.[1]

Four form critics have been most influential in Gospel studies. K. L. Schmidt was the first form critic of the Gospels; sadly, his major work—the most conservative and exegetically oriented of the earliest studies—has never been translated into English.[2] M. Dibelius is known for his attempt to show the preaching context of early Jesus traditions.[3] R. Bultmann is the most influential of all form critics. Despite his scepticism, Bultmann has painstakingly

---

1. For more complete analyses, see R. H. Stein, *The Synoptic Problem* (Grand Rapids: Baker, 1987), 161–228; E. V. McKnight, *What Is Form Criticism?* (Philadelphia: Fortress, 1969).

2. K. L. Schmidt, *Der Rahmen der Geschichte Jesu: Literarkritische Untersuchungen zur ältesten Jesusüberlieferung* (Berlin: Trowitzsch & Sohn, 1919).

3. M. Dibelius, *From Tradition to Gospel,* trans. by B. L. Woolf (London: Ivor Nicholson, 1934, = 1919).

classified virtually every Gospel saying and his classifications are often quite helpful. Even if put off by Bultmann's methodological scepticism, the serious student will read large portions of his work.[4] Finally, V. Taylor made the discipline of form criticism palatable to British scholarship and, indirectly, to more conservative wings.[5] His work remains helpful for all who want to do form criticism without undue scepticism.

Definition and Explanation

Form criticism is a discipline of historians designed to uncover from written traditions underlying oral traditions which were transmitted in given forms under certain laws of transmission and utilized in specific church contexts. Several considerations follow.

First, form criticism begins with written traditions and infers oral traditions, usually by eliminating the author's style.[6] It is essential to recognize that the evangelists were not just authors; they were transmitters (see Matt. 15:2–6; 1 Cor. 11:23; 15:1–8; 2 Thess. 2:15; Jude 3).

Second, form criticism assumes that there were oral traditions. That traditions were passed on orally is supported both from Judaism, known for its interest in and ability to pass on traditions orally, as well as from Papias, who states quite explicitly that he is more concerned with the "living voice" than the written one.[7]

Third, form criticism assumes that these oral traditions were passed on in forms that regulated the transmission process. Scholars have used different categories for the same essential form. (See table 5 for examples; Dibelius's and Bultmann's terms are drawn from Graeco-Roman categories.[8])

---

4. R. Bultmann, *The History of the Synoptic Tradition*, trans. by J. Marsh (New York: Harper & Row, 1963, = 1921).

5. V. Taylor, *The Formation of the Gospel Tradition* (London: Macmillan, 1968).

6. This aspect of inference has been rigorously worked out by B. D. Chilton, *God in Strength: Jesus' Announcement of the Kingdom* (Freistadt: F. Plöchl, 1979).

7. Eusebius, *Church History*, 3.39.1–7.

8. For a more complete explanation and chart, see Stein, *Synoptic Problem*, 168–74.

Table 5

Formal Categories

Dibelius	Bultmann	Taylor
Paradigms	Apophthegms	Pronouncement
Tales (Novellen)	Miracle Stories	Miracle Stories
Legends	Historical Stories	Stories About Jesus
Myths	Legends	
Paränesis	Dominical Sayings	Sayings and Parables
Unclassified	Miscellaneous	

Fourth, form criticism assumes that these oral traditions were passed on according to some basic laws of transmission: (1) a tendency to *expand* (Matt. 16:13–23; Mark 8:27–33); (2) a tendency to *clarify or elaborate details* (Mark 14:13; Luke 22:8); and (3) a tendency to *reduce Semitisms* (Matt. 10:37; Luke 14:26).

Fifth, form criticism assumes that these oral traditions were transmitted unconnected. Earlier form critics operated with the assumption that the present connections in the Gospels were made completely by the early church and the Evangelists; they assumed that the Evangelists were largely "cutting out traditions" and "pasting them together" without regard to, or knowledge of, historical connections.

Sixth, form criticism assumes that these traditions were passed on to meet various needs of the early churches. Thus, the stories we find were meaningful and therefore transmitted.

Seventh, form criticism attempts to specify which church contexts served to develop these forms. A form critic will analyze a given story in the Gospels, postulate a typical early church setting (e.g., worship, preaching, instruction, Lord's Supper) in which the given story was most likely developed, and, with circular reasoning, then see what that tradition tells us about that setting.[9]

Eighth, form criticism often asserts that the contents of the forms were determined largely by the needs of the churches. The classic statement of this is Bultmann's:

---

9. A helpful introduction to the New Testament in light of the types of settings from which various elements would have arisen is C. F. D. Moule, *The Birth of the New Testament*, 3d ed. (San Francisco: Harper & Row, 1981).

The proper understanding of form-criticism rests upon the judge-
ment that the literature in which the life of a given community, even
the primitive Christian community, has taken shape, *springs out of*
quite definite conditions and wants of life *from which grows up* a quite
definite style and quite specific forms and categories. Thus every
literary category has its 'life situation' (*Sitz im Leben:* Gunkel),
whether it be worship in its different forms, or work, or hunting, or
war. The *Sitz im Leben* is not, however, an individual historical event,
but a typical situation or occupation in the life of a community.[10]

Basic "Forms" of Form Criticism

The following forms for Gospel exegesis are standard. One becomes adept at identifying them only by practicing form criticism:
examining various passages in the Synoptics, classifying them by
form, and then reading each in light of that classification to get the
feel for what the form critics are doing.

Pronouncement stories are short sayings of Jesus found in brief
contexts such as controversy (Mark 2:23–28), theological dialogue
(Mark 12:38–44), and biography (Luke 9:57–62). The importance of
this "form" is that the story is told for the sake of the saying, not the
saying for the story. This means that one must look carefully for
dramatic elements which climax in a pronouncement by Jesus.
Observe the formal elements of Mark 2:23–28: a controversial action (2:23), the condemnation of the Pharisees (2:24), interrogation
by Jesus (2:25–26), and Jesus' pungent pronouncement (2:27–28).
The ὥστε of 2:28 sounds the final victory of Jesus.

Dominical sayings are short sayings of Jesus, with or without
contexts. This "formless form" groups together the sayings of
Jesus—even those found in pronouncement stories. For the sayings of Jesus one needs to discover, through the margin references
in Nestle-Aland, concordances, and commentaries, other sayings
which are fully or partially parallel in form. Then, through comparison, observations need to be made, asking what type of setting
gave rise to this form, whether there are variations from this form,
and so on. It is often the case that no true formal parallels will be

---

10. Bultmann, *Synoptic Tradition*, 4; emphasis added.

found; however, when parallels are found, they usually generate fresh insights for old sayings. For example, there are "I have come" sayings as well as "the Son of Man has come" sayings. Are there textual, historical, redactional, or polemical factors which predominate in one of these types?

Bultmann used the following categories for dominical sayings, most of which have proved both helpful and accurate:[11]

Logia: Jesus as the Teacher of Wisdom (69–108);

Prophetic and Apocalyptic Sayings (108–30);

Legal Sayings and Church Rules (130–50);

"I" Sayings (150–63);

Similitudes and Similar Forms (166–205).

Miracle stories are stories in which a miracle is the central thrust and is often described in detail (e.g., Mark 4:35–41).[12] A miracle story is normally structured as follows: the impossibility of the situation is described (Luke 5:12a); the one in need approaches Jesus in faith (Luke 5:12b); Jesus then responds, sometimes in dialogue, sometimes with a miraculous cure (Luke 5:13); after the miracle occurs, either Jesus issues commands (Luke 5:14–15), the crowds marvel (Mark 1:27) or the narrator offers an evaluation (Matt. 8:13b). But whatever the additional motifs, miracle stories, by nature, focus on Jesus—his ability to overcome impossible odds by assaulting earthly limitations with kingdom forces. Put simply, though miracle stories often contain expressions of faith and praise, they are not trying to teach us about those things. We are not taught by the healing of the paralytic any more to dig through a roof than we are by Jesus' calming of the storm to take catnaps in a

---

11. The numbers in parentheses refer to pages in Bultmann's *The History of the Synoptic Tradition*.

12. See G. Theissen, *The Miracle Stories of the Early Christian Tradition*, trans. F. McDonagh (Philadelphia: Fortress, 1983). Theissen identifies thirty-three motifs (e.g., coming of miracle worker, falling to knees, touch, prayer) and six themes (exorcisms, healings, epiphanies, rescue miracles, gift miracles, rule miracles). He then examines some of the possibilities of miracle stories through diverse combinations of the above factors.

boat! Miracle stories concentrate their energies on Jesus; the interpreter becomes accurate when their formal nature is respected.

Form critics classify the more supernatural, religiously edifying stories about Jesus as *historical stories*. These have often been called "legends" or "myths" because of the heavy element of the supernatural. Included here are the baptism, the temptation, the transfiguration, the temple incident (Luke 2:41–51), and the triumphal entry (Mark 11:1–10). As with dominical sayings, this category is not a clear "form"; instead, it groups together the most stupendous events in the life of Jesus.

The *passion narrative* (Mark 10–16) is generally regarded as a pre-Gospel literary unit. The "formal" value of the passion narrative is limited. Further, within the passion narrative are an assortment of other forms (pronouncements, dominical sayings, miracle stories, and historical stories).

These scholars and ideas associated with form criticism have provoked stiff criticism from New Testament scholars. Though form criticism is both valuable and necessary for exegesis of the Synoptics, it has its limitations and is greatly influenced—perhaps more than any other method of synoptic studies—by one's presuppositions. We need to look at the criticisms of this discipline before we make some statements about its value for exegesis.

Negative Evaluation of Form Criticism

First, it is a mistake to assume that stories in the Synoptics cannot reflect a "mixed" form (e.g., a miracle story may also have a pronouncement element).

Second, the presence of both eyewitnesses and apostles seriously curtails the creativity of the early church despite the form critic's insistence that sayings were invented. There is clear evidence in the early church (e.g., 1 Cor. 7:10, 12) that a distinction was made between Christian decisions and the decisions of the historical Jesus.[13]

---

13. That the early church had a historical consciousness has been demonstrated by B. F. Meyer, *Aims of Jesus* (London: SCM, 1979), 60–75. See Stein, *Synoptic Problem*, 188–92; on eyewitnesses, see 193–203.

Third, it is recognized more and more that Jesus taught with a view to his sayings being repeated and remembered by his followers.[14] B. Gerhardsson offers cogent arguments for Jesus being the authoritative teacher for the church from the very beginning; he taught the Twelve carefully and, at times, in ways that were easily memorizable. If this be the case, and there is no compelling reason to deny it, memorization capacity weakens the proposal of creation and strengthens the case of reliability.

Fourth, as E. P. Sanders pointed out, to speak of "laws" of transmission is inaccurate. Consequently, form criticism will have to accept a greater flexibility in how material was passed on if it is to remain true to the stuff of history. Scholars are becoming more and more convinced that a simple development from orality to textuality is in fact overly simplistic; there appears to have been a contemporary transmission of the Jesus traditions in both oral and textual forms.[15]

Fifth, it is illogical to assume that forms determine contents as has been done so regularly. This is the worst sort of circular argument: the present saying would fit in an apologetic context; therefore, it came from the early church's apologetics efforts; therefore, it was created for this apologetic context; therefore, because it came from an apologetic context, it did not come from Jesus. Such questionable logic confronts the reader far too frequently in form-critical works. For example, in discussing the plucking of corn on the Sabbath, Bultmann offers the following comments: "The point is that Sabbath-breaking to satisfy hunger is defended on scriptural grounds. The composition—defence by counter-question—is *stylistic*. But the *composition* is the work of the Church: Jesus is questioned about the disciples' behaviour; *why not about his own?*

---

14. See B. Gerhardsson, *The Origins of the Gospel Traditions* (Philadelphia: Fortress, 1977), 19–24. Stein, following H. Schürmann, proposes the mission of the Twelve as the most likely *Sitz im Leben* for the conception of the Jesus traditions (*Synoptic Problem*, 203–5).

15. See L. R. Keylock, "Bultmann's Law of Increasing Distinctness," in *Current Issues in Biblical and Patristic Interpretation: Studies in Honor of Merrill C. Tenney Presented by His Former Students*, ed. by G. F. Hawthorne, 193–210 (Grand Rapids: Eerdmans, 1975); E. P. Sanders, *The Tendencies of the Synoptic Tradition*, Society for New Testament Studies Monograph Series, no. 9 (Cambridge: Cambridge University Press, 1969); W. H. Kelber, *The Oral and Written Gospel* (Philadelphia: Fortress, 1983).

i.e. the Church ascribes the justification of her Sabbath customs to Jesus."[16]
The logic here is patently circular!

Sixth, from the very beginning the assumption that the individual pericopae were passed on unconnected has been challenged, in particular, by C. H. Dodd.[17] This represents a serious challenge to form criticism and should not be overlooked. Dodd argues that there were different types of material in the Gospels: independent units, larger complexes, and a basic outline of the life of Jesus. This latter aspect can be glimpsed in the so-called Markan summaries (1:14–15, 21–22, 39; 3:7b–19; 4:33–34; 6:7, 12–13, 30) as well as in the early sermons in Acts (2:14–39; 3:13–26; 4:10–12; 5:30–32; 10:37–41; 13:17–41).

The above criticisms not only offer a challenge to form criticism but, in many ways, undermine and seriously restrict its value for accomplishing what it seeks to accomplish—to write a history of the early church by way of inference from the synoptic narratives. These criticisms are so methodologically sound that the only abiding interpretative value of form criticism is its classification of the Gospel material into various "forms." The irony is that what began as an attempt to describe "orality" has turned mostly into a legacy of "textuality." This is not surprising because the early form critics were students of the texts themselves and, so, their observations were almost always textually determined. We turn then to the literary and historical values of the enterprise.

Positive Evaluation of Form Criticism

First, form criticism, when used properly, may shed light on the period of oral transmission, and therefore shorten the time span between Jesus and the records of Jesus. However, an important caution must be raised: even when used properly (without excessive scepticism), all we can know about the early church is by way of inference. For example, one might infer that discussions of the Sabbath in the Gospels reflect the early church's attempt to deal

---

16. Bultmann, *Synoptic Tradition*, 16; emphasis added.
17. C. H. Dodd, "The Framework of the Gospel Narrative," *Expository Times* 43 (1932): 396–400.

with the presence of Gentiles among Jews and the problem this caused for Sabbath practices. Although this is possible and the type of thing we might expect to occur, it is by no means proven by the presence of such stories. However, if such inferences seem compelling at times, they will shorten the time span between Jesus and the canonical Gospels and thereby provide valuable historical information.[18]

Second, form critics force all historians to recognize that the Evangelists wrote their Gospels from a definite point of view with definite purposes: Jesus was the Messiah, the Lord, and they were exhorting their readers to believe and obey him. Form criticism has definitely aided New Testament scholarship by drawing attention to these "faith tendencies" of the Gospel writers. As William Barclay notes: "An historian cannot simply relate the facts; he must pass some kind of judgment upon them. . . . And this necessarily involves a standpoint from which such a judgment can be made. . . . To demand history in detachment is both an impossibility and a contradiction in terms."[19] The Evangelists wrote from a theological vantage point.

Finally, the most significant contribution of form criticism has been the minute examination of the evidence in order to find "forms." Consequently, we gain in interpretative skills as we learn more about the various methods of Jesus and the Evangelists in speaking and teaching. We will know that a given passage is a pronouncement story, not a miracle story, and that we must interpret it from that angle to be fair to the text. In scrupulously categorizing the synoptic forms, form critics have provided an invaluable set of grids (various forms) which enable the student to see the basic structure of a given story or saying. Each grid (or form) demands a separate sensitivity.

Examples of Form Criticism

In closing, we shall look at a few examples of form criticism. A common form to which the student must accustom himself is the

---

18. For a recent (and cautious) study in this direction, see J. D. G. Dunn, "Mark 2.1–3.6: A Bridge Between Jesus and Paul on the Question of the Law," *New Testament Studies* 30 (1984): 395–415.

19. W. Barclay, *Introduction to the First Three Gospels* (Philadelphia: Westminster, 1975), 20.

pronouncement story. An example is Mark 3:31–35. This short story climaxes in a saying of Jesus. The whole story (so it is argued by form critics) was preserved because the saying was meaningful for the church. When some people alert Jesus to the presence of his family (v. 32), Jesus makes a pronouncement on the nature of the true family of God: ὃς [γὰρ] ἂν ποιήσῃ τὸ θέλημα τοῦ θεοῦ, οὗτος ἀδελφός μου καὶ ἀδελφὴ καὶ μήτηρ ἐστίν (v. 35). There is no reason to doubt that this story was remembered for this climactic saying, and was probably told to meet certain needs in the early church, such as struggles over the lack of faith in parents and family (cf. Matt. 10:21, 34–39; 1 Peter 3:1–6). During such struggles, this saying of Jesus would be particularly comforting. But the point is that our attention must be focused on the evaluative comment by Jesus on the nature of the true people of God. The entire story is to be understood from that angle.[20]

A second example is a miracle story. Matthew 9:27–31 represents a typical miracle story: Jesus encounters a situation of great need (blindness); he is petitioned for healing; Jesus probes for faith and, when it is clear that the needy do believe, his healing powers are unleashed. In spite of his warning not to make this miracle known, the two blind men spread the news throughout the land, their action functioning as a commentary on the glorious power of Jesus. The point of the story, made more effective by a "miracle form" (insoluble problem, Jesus' presence, faith, healing, comment), is the power of Jesus and the response to him. To construe this story as a way of teaching how to obtain faith or to turn it into a parable of salvation (as so many evangelicals are prone to do) is to mis-interpret what is patently a miracle story about Jesus' ability to unveil kingdom power when people believe in him.[21]

A final example comes from sayings of Jesus, where the inves-tigation of form critics has been remarkably insightful. For example, Matthew 5:17–20 is composed of four types (forms) of sayings of

---

20. See Bultmann, *Synoptic Tradition*, 29–31. Bultmann argues that verses 31–34 are "imaginary" and were created for verse 35. See criticisms of Bultmann in Taylor, *Mark*, 245.

21. Dibelius believes that this story was created by Matthew (*From Tradition to Gospel*, 42) while Bultmann maintains that it developed under the influence of the Markan pattern. On the patterns of healing miracles, see *Synoptic Tradition*, 209–15. See also Theissen, *Miracle Stories*, 43–121; Stein, *Synoptic Problem*, 170–71.

Jesus: (1) an "I have come" saying (cf. also 9:13; 10:34–35); (2) an "Amen" saying (cf. also 5:26; 10:23; 16:28; 23:39; 24:34; 26:29); (3) a "sentence of holy law," or an early church rule for practice (cf. also 10:32–33); and (4) an "entrance" saying (cf. 7:21; 18:3; 19:23–24; 23:13). Apart from the need to interpret each of these sayings in context, no one who investigates the "formal parallels" mentioned above (and others throughout the synoptic tradition could be added) can doubt the usefulness of seeing the sayings of Jesus according to their various forms.

Each of these kinds of dominical sayings has unique patterns, variations from which are often significant for interpretation. Notice, for instance, the entrance saying. We find that Jesus regularly expressed what one had to do in order to enter the kingdom of heaven and, rather than expressing that one must do this *and* this *and* this, the "form" shows that Jesus could substitute various images into the same form without changing the general demand (i.e., radical surrender to the will of God in trust and obedience). Thus, one must do the will of God (Matt. 7:21), turn and become like a child (Matt. 18:3), abandon riches (Matt. 19:21), and not follow the Pharisees (Matt. 23:13).

It is often the case that formal parallels keep us from misunderstanding what Jesus means. In this case, one should not then think that Jesus teaches a works righteousness, though one might infer that from Matthew 7:21. It is of utmost importance that, in interpreting the synoptic Gospels, one carefully notes "formal" considerations of the sayings of Jesus. If one wants to explore this further, each of the four "forms" in Matthew 5:17–20 can be profitably explored for variation and implication, asking questions such as what Jesus came to do (5:17), what factors gave rise to an "Amen" saying (5:18), and what kinds of legislated factors are in "sentences of holy law."[22]

This completes our analysis and evaluation of form criticism, the second stop on the route "from Jesus to the canonical text." Its

---

22. See R. A. Guelich, *The Sermon on the Mount: A Foundation for Understanding* (Waco, Tex.: Word, 1982), 134–74. A brief discussion is found on 134–36; however, the implications of form-critical analysis are evident thereafter.

ultimate benefit for exegesis is classification of the various forms in the Synoptics and the light that this sheds on the text. We shall next examine how the Evangelists handled the traditions to see what light such editorial activity sheds on the texts.

8

Tradition Analysis
Redaction Criticism

The ultimate concern of tradition-critical analysis is to trace the history of a given pericope, to discern the event or saying which lay at the foundation, to follow its transmission through oral and written stages, and, finally, to examine what each Evangelist has done to that tradition in order to understand the text itself.[1] That not all scholars have come "full circle" should not denigrate the method itself. This chapter will seek to explain and evaluate the tool which is most concerned with the final layer of the text: redaction criticism.

K. L. Schmidt emphasized the "scissors, paste and glue" nature of the Gospels. Procedurally, form critics eliminate the glue and then try to locate a given tradition in an early Christian setting. Redaction criticism, through the aid of both form and source criti-

---

1. See R. H. Stein, "What Is Redaktionsgeschichte?" *Journal of Biblical Literature* 88 (1969): 45–56; N. Perrin, *What Is Redaction Criticism?* (Philadelphia: Fortress, 1974). For a survey of early redaction criticism of the synoptic Gospels, see J. Rhode, *Rediscovering the Teaching of the Evangelists,* trans. by D. M. Barton (Philadelphia: Westminster, 1968).

For evangelical perspectives on redaction criticism, see G. R. Osborne, "The Evangelical and Redaction Criticism," *Journal of the Evangelical Theological Society* 22 (1979): 305–22; D. A. Carson, "Redaction Criticism: On the Legitimacy and Illegitimacy of a Literary Tool," in D. A. Carson and J. D. Woodbridge, *Scripture and Truth,* 119–42 (Grand Rapids: Zondervan, 1983); R. H. Stein, *The Synoptic Problem* (Grand Rapids: Baker, 1987), 231–72.

cism, seeks to remedy the overemphasis in form criticism on pre-textual factors by focusing concern on the "glue" itself. So redaction criticism seeks to determine what the redactor (editor) did to the tradition.

In this chapter we will explain redaction criticism, noting the earliest critics and then evaluating its weaknesses and strengths, seeking to discover what contribution redaction criticism makes to the exegetical task.

Definition and Analysis

Redaction criticism is a discipline of historians designed to un-cover from a written source the particular contributions of an au-thor to the traditions he utilized in order better to understand his theological viewpoint and setting. Several inferences can be drawn from this definition.

First, redaction criticism assumes the existence of written sources and seeks to discover the contributions (redactional altera-tions) of the Evangelists to those sources. For example, a redaction critic, usually assuming Markan priority, inquires into the nature of and rationale for Matthew's addition of Peter's unsuccessful attempt to walk on the water (cf. Mark 6:45–52 with Matt. 14:22–33). The critic seeks to discover whether the confession at the end of the story (Matt. 14:33) is materially different from Mark's rather nega-tive comment (Mark 6:52).[2]

Second, redaction criticism is concerned with the theological motivation for these alterations. Redaction critics seek to know *why* Luke (or Matthew) has changed Mark. When a change is dis-covered, redaction critics look elsewhere to see if this change is typical for that Evangelist and if patterns of thought emerge from these changes. For example, redaction critics examine Matthew for other incidents involving Peter to see if a consistent pattern can be detected. Of course, Matthew does have a consistent interest in

_____

2. Redaction criticism of Mark is a much more speculative process. See. E. J. Pryke, *Redactional Style in the Marcan Gospel: A Study of Syntax and Vocabulary as Guides to Redaction in Mark,* Society for New Testament Studies Monograph Series, no. 33 (Cambridge: Cambridge University Press, 1978).

Peter as the leader of the apostolic band, both as representative and leader.

Third, redaction criticism is concerned with composing a theology of each Evangelist. Not only does it take individual alterations into view, it also studies the patterns of changes throughout a given Gospel to see if an overall theology can be detected. In fact, the development of redaction criticism's interest—from minute alterations unique to an Evangelist as compared with his inherited traditions to larger patterns (including literary strategies)—has sometimes been called "composition criticism." Technically, such a distinction can be drawn; practically, however, there are few treatments which do not utilize both procedures together. In using the term *redaction criticism*, then, we are referring to both aspects.

Finally, redaction criticism is concerned with the early church setting in which the theological viewpoint of an Evangelist can best be explained. A redaction critic may go so far as to suggest a *Sitz im Leben* from which the Evangelist's own views emerged, for example, the so-called "delay of the Parousia" or intense debates with Judaism over the place of the Law.

Having defined and explained the major elements of redaction criticism, we need to survey briefly the major redaction critics. But before we do this, an overview of the types of redaction which scholars have discovered through careful analyses of the Synoptics will be presented.

Redactional Activity

When scholars speak of "redaction," what sorts of editorial activity by the Evangelists do they have in mind? There are at least seven important characteristics of that editorial activity.

First, the most obvious kind of redaction is, in fact, "nonredaction"—conservation. The predominant form of editing the Evangelists practiced was simply passing on the traditions which they had before them. A classic example, which illustrates both conservation and the interdependence of the Synoptics, is the choice of both Matthew and Luke to conserve Mark's parenthetical comment, thereby forcing an incomplete sentence (see Mark 2:10; Matt. 9:6; Luke 5:24).

Second, the Evangelists at times conflate two traditions. A not uncommon feature of the Byzantine text type is the conflation of two separate readings; the same thing can be found in the synoptic Gospels when an author chooses to utilize two traditions of the same event or saying. Thus, when Matthew and Luke record the temptation of Jesus, it is clear that they begin with Mark (cf. Matt. 4:1–2; Luke 4:1–2) and then complete the story with Q (cf. Matt. 4:3–11; Luke 4:3–13).

A third type of redaction, related to conflation, is expansion (adding a different tradition or explaining another tradition with a gloss). For example, in Luke 1–2 we see a major expansion of the Markan outline, and in Matthew 4:12–16 Matthew expands a brief summary of Mark (1:14) with a reflection on Old Testament fulfillment. (For clarification, expansion differs from conflation in that it is used when two traditions of the same event or saying are combined.)

Fourth, scholars often point to transpositions of traditions in the Synoptics; that is, what is found in one location in Mark, Luke, or Matthew is found in a different setting in another Gospel. Jesus' compassion for Jerusalem is found at the end of the woes in Matthew (23:37–39), but occurs in a completely different context in Luke (13:34–35)—and few scholars doubt that this is a transposition. When it comes to the sayings of Jesus, students will want to decide whether Jesus repeated himself in two different settings or whether the Evangelists have chosen to transpose a saying from one setting to another. To rule out either option at the outset is to prejudge the matter.

Fifth, one Evangelist will regularly choose for a variety of reasons to omit what is found in his traditions. Whereas Matthew chooses to omit Mark's comment about digging through a roof to get to Jesus (cf. Mark 2:4; Matt. 8:2), Luke chooses to conserve it (Luke 5:19). Occasionally, the omission is made simply to avoid redundancy (cf. Mark 2:15 with Luke 5:29).

A sixth type of redaction is explication, that is, one Evangelist will choose to explain a given fact in a tradition, as when Mark draws out the implication of a Jewish practice (7:3–4) or an action of Jesus (Mark 7:19), or when Matthew changes "Son of Man" to "I" (cf. Luke 12:8; Matt. 10:32). Perhaps a bit of humor can be seen in Luke's reexplanation of the doctor's practices and abilities (cf. Mark 5:26; Luke 8:43).

Finally, a common feature of redaction is alteration. In one sense, most of the above types of redaction are alterations. This final example, however, involves direct alterations of the tradition to avoid misunderstandings, as when Matthew alters Mark's comment which could suggest inability on the part of Jesus (Mark 6:5; Matt. 13:58) or when he changes Mark's form of address by the rich young ruler (Mark 10:17–18; Matt. 19:16–17). Another type of alteration appears to have "formal" motivations (cf. Matt. 7:21 with Luke 6:46).

Redaction criticism, as mentioned before, is the use of form and source criticism to clarify the Evangelists' contributions. And, although such observations have been around since Augustine, who spoke clearly of the christological (redactional) tendencies of the Evangelists (see *Harmony* 1:2–6), it was not until after World War II that the discipline was worked out methodologically.

Major Catalysts in Redaction Criticism

Scholarship is in almost universal agreement that the beginning of redaction criticism is to be found in the works of H. Conzelmann, W. Marxsen, and G. Bornkamm,[3] three German university professors; we will briefly survey their early efforts.

G. Bornkamm was the first to apply a conscious redaction-critical method to Matthew. His essay, "The Stilling of the Storm in Matthew," marks a watershed in Matthean scholarship.[4] Bornkamm's concern was to show that Matthew's report of the

---

3. A case has been made for Ned Stonehouse as the first of redaction critics by M. Silva, "Ned B. Stonehouse and Redaction Criticism. Part I: The Witness of the Synoptic Evangelists to Christ. Part II: The Historicity of the Synoptic Tradition," *Westminster Theological Journal* 40 (1977–1978): 77–88, 281–303. See N. B. Stonehouse, *The Witness of the Synoptic Gospels to Christ* (Grand Rapids: Baker, 1979). One could make a similar case for W. Wrede (*The Messianic Secret*, trans. by J. C. G. Greig [Cambridge: James Clarke, 1971, =1901]) or R. H. Lightfoot (*History and Interpretation in the Gospels*, The Bampton Lectures of 1934 [New York: Harper and Bros., n.d.]). A helpful survey can be found in Perrin, *What Is Redaction Criticism?*, 1–39.

4. G. Bornkamm, "The Stilling of the Storm in Matthew," in *Tradition and Interpretation in Matthew*, ed. by G. Bornkamm, G. Barth, and H. J. Held, trans. by P. Scott, 52–57 (Philadelphia: Westminster, 1974).

stilling of the storm has a totally different meaning than the report in Mark. Matthew, by subtle rearrangement and alteration, tells the story to emphasize both the danger and the glory of discipleship. The additional essays and dissertations published in *Tradition and Interpretation in Matthew* are the foundation for Matthean redactional studies.

H. Conzelmann argued that Luke wrote his Gospel to show that the time of the church is indefinite and that God works in distinct stages in history. Luke, he argues, was propelled to this view of history because of the delay of the Parousia.[5]

W. Marxsen's *Mark the Evangelist: Studies on the Redaction History of the Gospel* formed the impulse for Markan redactional analysis. In fact, he first used the term *Redaktionsgeschichte* ("redaction criticism"). After an analysis of John the Baptist, geographical terms, the term *gospel*, and Mark 13, Marxsen concludes that Mark wrote his Gospel to encourage Christians who had fled from Jerusalem to Galilee to await the Parousia at the outset of the Jewish War (A.D. 66).[6] Thus by a careful analysis of the redactional touches of Mark, the author "reads off" a *Sitz im Leben* in order better to elucidate the text of Mark. This concern with *Sitz im Leben* has become a dominant aspect of redaction criticism.

It ought to be said at this point, not in disparagement of these works but in honor of them, that hardly any scholars today agree with the basic theories of the early redaction critics. Rather, owing to their catalytic scholarship, modern redaction critics have taken up the methods of Bornkamm, Conzelmann, and Marxsen, refined them, and moved on to more permanent examinations of the redactional ideas of the Evangelists. In this process of refinement and reexamination, many criticisms have been leveled against redaction criticism. Before we can appropriate the method, we must understand its problems.

Negative Evaluation of Redaction Criticism

Students of the Synoptics all agree that redactional activity on the part of each of the synoptic Evangelists took part. This means

5. H. Conzelmann, *The Theology of St. Luke*, trans. by G. Buswell (New York: Harper & Row, 1960, =1954).

6. W. Marxsen, *Mark the Evangelist: Studies on the Redaction History of the Gospel*, trans. by J. Boyce, D. Juel, W. Poehlmann, and R. A. Harrisville (Nashville: Abingdon, 1969, =1956).

that it is fundamentally wrong not to do redactional analysis as one exegetes a synoptic passage. However, this does not mean that redaction critics do not need to ask some penetrating questions about their methods.

The most obvious problem is the initial uncertainties which naturally arise. By definition, this discipline requires that one isolate sources and redactional alterations. But we can never be absolutely certain about some of these matters since we can never be totally confident of a solution to the Synoptic Problem. Can we ever be sure that Matthew has composed the Peter incident in chapter 14?

This problem, however, merits a rejoinder. When there is a near majority on the Markan hypothesis, many uncertainties can be removed. That is, in some cases, such as when Matthew or Luke is using Mark or when a Q tradition is obvious, we can trace quite accurately just what these later Evangelists have done to Mark. One cannot have absolute certainty in these matters; nor should one expect to before proceeding. Further, one's confidence is strengthened when a discernible pattern emerges, as when Luke consistently calls attention to the "unlikely."

A second problem pertains to the detection of the motivations of the Evangelists. Though one can at times discern a pattern of redactional activity, it is difficult to probe further into the motivation of the author for producing such a pattern. Inferences as to motivations can almost never go beyond suggestions and are especially vulnerable to the charge of subjectivity. Anyone who has scanned a survey of suggested *Sitze im Leben* knows that scholars rarely agree in these matters. To follow through with a previous example, though we can be somewhat confident that Matthew has added the Peter story and that there is a pattern of addition in that Gospel, our ability to detect Matthew's motivations is restricted to little more than guesswork. C. S. Lewis, in commenting on the attempt of historians to guess the motivations of authors, painfully rebukes many redactional studies: "What I think I can say with certainty is that they are usually wrong."[7]

Third, we consider redaction criticism's ability to pronounce historical judgments. It is regularly stated that what is considered to be redactional is unhistorical. The logic of this is clear; if it is redactional, it is also unhistorical, because redaction is creation. But this

---

7. C. S. Lewis, *Christian Reflections*, ed. by W. Hooper (Grand Rapids: Eerdmans, 1967), 160.

is unacceptable. Redaction is a judgment of style; for example, this word or sentence is Luke's style. But to judge this as therefore unhistorical means that everything is unhistorical because every record is in someone's style. Furthermore, theology and history are not necessarily opposites. Again, if Matthew added the story about Peter, is it therefore unhistorical—simply because we detect it to be recorded in Matthew's style? Surely this is contorted historiography and logic! Redaction criticism has received unfavorable press because of the tendency of redaction critics to use faulty logic at precisely this point. The decision that something is redactional (and a case can often be reasonably made to argue this) is a conclusion regarding style, not history. Historical reliability must be decided on grounds both more secure and subtle than grammar and style.[8]

Fourth, we need to look at the frequent problem of interpretative priority. It is too frequently stated or assumed that what is important for interpreting Luke is to discover first what is redactional, then to eliminate what is traditional as of little use (i.e., unless it is unique to Luke, it is unimportant to him). Now the problem with this is simple: had Luke (or Matthew or Mark) not agreed with a given statement, had Luke preferred another word over one before him, and so on, he could have altered or omitted it. That he chose to retain a given tradition is tacit evidence that that tradition conveys the ideas which he also wants to convey. Certainly Luke's ability to omit proves that he was far from a slave to his traditions. Put a different way, one cannot give exclusive interpretative priority to the redactional elements in a given tradition. With respect to Matthew 14:22–33, then, one should not look just to the Peter incident or to the confession at the end. Rather, the entire episode must be analyzed as a unit. Granted, these "redactional" parts are

---

8. G. B. Caird pungently comments:

Redaction criticism treat [sic] the evangelists as interpreters, but all too often with the tacit assumption that to interpret is to misinterpret. Considering that they are themselves professional interpreters, it might seem wiser to allow for the possibility that an interpreter should occasionally be right. ("Study of the Gospels. III. Redaction Criticism," *Expository Times* 87 [1976]: 172)

helpful and often hermeneutically significant, but there is more to the story than what is "not underlined." Thus, we look for an Evangelist's views in everything that he says, taking some of our cues from how he has altered the tradition.

A further warning should be added at this point: one should not conclude that there is a theological motivation for every change. Because Matthew alters a Markan paratactic construction may mean nothing; perhaps the use of parataxis was more suitable to Mark than to Matthew. If the boon of redaction criticism is its careful attention to details, then its bane is its frequent (but mistaken) ability to shake redactional fruit from every bush!

A fifth problem is redaction criticism's tendency to find maximal diversity. Redaction criticism, as it is practiced today, looks for diversity between the Evangelists, seeking for divergent or even contradictory understandings. The older method, practiced in all historical disciplines, of seeking to harmonize parallel accounts, has been largely abandoned as precritical or naive. Again, the confession of Matthew 14:33 ("You are the Son of God") is seen by many redaction critics as flatly contradictory to Mark 6:52. Undoubtedly, differences are present, but this sort of difference can be harmonized in various ways, and harmonizations are not necessarily inferior.[9]

A final problem is that redaction critics too casually find creativity on the part of the Evangelists. It is regularly concluded in redactional studies that the Evangelists created sayings of Jesus. But the means of arriving at this conclusion is usually the same vicious cycle noted above, namely, that a given statement is stylistically Lukan and therefore a Lukan creation. Undoubtedly, clarifications, expansions, adaptations, explanations, glosses, and the like took place; but to argue that Mark, Matthew, or Luke invented a saying of Jesus requires more than vocabulary statistics. How frequently we operate with our personal paraphrases of scholars, preachers,

---

9. On harmonization as an important hermeneutical device, see the judicious article of C. L. Blomberg, "The Legitimacy and Limits of Harmonization," in *Hermeneutics, Authority, and Canon,* ed. by D. A. Carson and J. D. Woodbridge, 139–74 (Grand Rapids: Zondervan, 1986).

historians, and even our spouses—and yet one is never accused of creating information in doing this!

Positive Evaluation of Redaction Criticism

It is clear that redaction took place; of this there can be no doubt. The authors did not simply copy the words of Jesus. The Gospels show too much diversity to think simply in terms of copying, and too many of these alterations are found consistently in each Gospel. Furthermore, it is entirely reasonable to conclude that consistent patterns in a Gospel reflect the personal views of its author. Consequently, it is incumbent upon the Gospel interpreter to concentrate seriously on the redactional contours of the text. What value will such a procedure have for interpretation?

First, in contrast to form criticism, redaction criticism emphasizes the author of a Gospel. While examination of the oral and written traditions which preceded the canonical text is interesting and indeed has a place in the exegetical procedure, the ultimate goal of exegesis is to make sense of the author's intended meaning and this is what redaction criticism does.

Second, the most important contribution of the redaction-critical method is precision in interpretation. Redaction criticism's ability to sharpen the precise meaning of the author by noting his subtle alterations and stresses enables us to interpret more accurately the intended meaning of the author. The lines which are not underlined in a synopsis are potential clues to Luke's intention in recording a saying or event. One ought to work through such clues carefully.

At this point one may be tempted, quite naturally, to ask how Luke's audience was to perceive these subtleties. This is a good question and the answer to it is important. The quest of exegesis is to grasp the intention of the author, not the audience's perceptions of the author's intentions. Further, inspiration is the process of God working upon the *author*, not the audience. Finally, if Matthew and/or Luke were using Mark, then any alterations were intended by Matthew and Luke, and they, at least, had reasons for these. D. A. Carson observes: "The one place where redaction criticism may offer considerably more help, and where it may function with

some legitimacy, is in aiding us to discern more closely the Evangelists' individual concerns and emphases."[10]

The Gospels must then be seen as two-edged: speaking about
Jesus (historical intention) to the Evangelists' congregations (eccle-
siological intention). Redaction criticism teaches us that our task is
not finished until we have prospected both fields.

Third, redaction criticism has helped us to clarify the nature of
the genre of the synoptic Gospels. If the criteria of tradition criticism pointed us to the referential nature of the Gospels, and consequently, led us to admit that the Gospels are historical and
biographical in nature, then redaction criticism suggests that the
historical orientation of the Gospels has been overlayed with keryg-
matic and didactic interests.[11] Thus, redaction criticism teaches us
to see that the Gospels are biographies about Jesus for the churches
in all their various needs. M. Silva notes: "In other words, our Lord
himself [through inspiration] has guided the evangelists as they
seek, *not only to report, but also to interpret and to apply* the life and
ministry of Jesus to their Christian communities."[12]

Finally, when exercising proper caution and humility, the redaction critic can often make suggestions about the nature of the early
churches. If suggestions of a given consistent redactional tendency
are even close approximations to a particular situation, then we can
make some progress in developing our understanding of earliest
Christianity. But, again, this can be done only with great discretion
and then, it might be added, it would be hazardous indeed to
utilize such suggestions as heuristic devices throughout the text. It
would be preferable to make such suggestions for the sake of historical understanding rather than for the sake of unearthing the
hidden nuances of a particular text.

We shall conclude with some observations about the use of this
tradition-critical process for exegesis. At this juncture, we intend to

---

10. Carson, "Redaction Criticism," 140.

11. This implication of redaction criticism has incited a good deal of discussion among evangelicals, ranging from R. H. Gundry's view of Matthew as a
midrash of early Christian traditions to heated rejection of the interpretative
element of the Evangelists. See the exchange between R. H. Gundry and D. J.
Moo concerning the issue of genre in the *Journal of the Evangelical Theological
Society* 26 (1983): 31–39, 41–56, 57–70, 71–86.

12. Silva, "Ned B. Stonehouse," 289.

give methodological suggestions for the entire tradition-critical process which we have been examining since chapter 6.

Methodological Suggestions Regarding Tradition Analysis

Until the interpreter has come to terms with the data themselves by carefully underlining a synopsis (this is most important) and an adequate solution to the Synoptic Problem has been obtained, a great deal of confusion will reign. After this has been done, the following methodological procedures are recommended.[13]

First, through the use of tradition-critical criteria (and other basic methods in history), the pericope needs to be examined to see if it reports historically reliable information. Evangelicals, of course, have tended to deny all "mythic" elements in the Gospels and for good reason. Evangelicals may eventually agree that some elements of narratives are parabolic in nature but until some methodologically sound criteria are developed, it appears that the tradition-critical criteria will have to be used for positive, not negative, purposes. And so the first step is to probe the individual genre of the pericope at hand, to see if it is historically reliable material.[14]

Second, after examining issues pertaining to historicity, the next step is to inquire into the formal nature of the story or saying. If it is a narrative, it must be decided if the story is a pronouncement story, a miracle story, or a historical story about Jesus (or a "mixed form"). If it is a saying, one needs to seek formal parallels. For each of these, minute comparative observations need to be

---

13. For an example of this process, see S. McKnight, "Jesus and the End-Time: Matthew 10:23," *Society of Biblical Literature Seminar Papers* (1986): 501–20. Though written for professional Gospel critics, it provides an example of tradition-critical analysis.

14. In this connection, R. H. Gundry contended that the magi were a midrashic convention of Matthew (2:1–12). On a priori grounds, evangelicals cannot condemn such a view as contrary to inspiration and inerrancy. The issue, however, is that our tools are not refined enough to make such a conclusion with sufficient confidence. See R. H. Gundry, *Matthew: A Commentary on His Literary and Theological Art* (Grand Rapids: Eerdmans, 1982), 26–32.

undertaken to see if such comparisons yield suggestive material for understanding a given pericope.

Third, form-critical analysis should give way to source-critical and redaction-critical observations. Here the student needs to ask about the source of each word or expression. It is often the case that no reasonable conclusion can be reached for given words and expressions; however, through careful comparison of a synopsis it is often the case that one can conclude with good reason that Matthew or Luke inherited this word or expression from Mark or that they have added/omitted/altered a given word. When one can trace such changes, further probing needs to take place. If a word (see next chapter) has been added, the student will want to see if an Evangelist consistently adds that word. If so, the student should observe whether any patterns become evident. If a given redactional element pertains to a theme, the student needs to compare carefully a given theme in one Gospel with that theme in another Gospel. Again, one is looking for patterns in order to see if they shed light on the individual pericope under analysis.

Where does one look for redactional elements? One can often locate literary strategies and themes in the beginnings and endings of pericopes (seams), summaries, insertions, and individual favorite words. In doing redactional analysis, what one is actually doing is carefully examining one Gospel in direct comparison to another. The process is indeed tedious, yet it is also often rewarding.

Fourth, the student is not finished until the results of a given pericope's analysis are absorbed into the context of that entire Gospel. After analyzing the parable of the prodigal son (Luke 15:11–32), for instance, one ought to ask what Luke says elsewhere about repentance and God's love for sinners. A thorough analysis of Luke on this theme, as often as possible in comparison both with Mark and Matthew, will shed light on his intention in Luke 15.

Finally, a tradition critic can conclude with observations about the historical setting out of which given redactional streams have emerged. If one desires to do so, this is the place where inferences should be made but one must be cautious.

Following textual, grammatical, and tradition-critical analyses of a given pericope, the student should be able to make a coherent, logical statement about the intention of the author for this text in its context. We shall now examine the special techniques for doing word and theme analysis in the Synoptics.

9

Word Analysis

Once the exegete has learned to underline a synopsis and to appreciate the three-dimensional nature of the Gospels, word studies can become a wondrous adventure. In synoptic word studies, the uniqueness of synoptic exegesis comes to the fore. For example, the student of the Synoptics may want to know if a particular word is a favorite of an individual author and, if so, how that author uses that particular word in passing on traditions. Does Luke, for instance, tend to add a term (e.g., δόξα), and if he does, what does he mean by it? Word studies can (or, should) become the investigation, not just of the generic lexical meaning of a term in the ancient world, but of the meaning of that term in an individual author and context. Put differently, synoptic word studies are concerned with the profile an author gives to a certain lexical unit. This chapter is concerned with word studies in general and their value for the synoptic Gospels in particular. Because the general aspect of word studies has been covered in the introductory volume, we will offer just a few comments and then plunge more deeply into the genius of synoptic word analysis.

Word studies in the Synoptics begin as do word studies in any work of ancient literature because the purpose of all word analysis is to determine both the denotative (largely synonymous to the lexical meaning) and connotative meaning of a given word. The standard approach to word studies is diachronic, studying the historical development of a term. More recently, however, scholars have become convinced that primary concentration should be focused instead on the synchronic meaning of a term, that is, what the particular word meant at a particular time in history (e.g., the Hellenistic era). Whereas a diachronic study may lead one to see that the meaning of the term *holy* developed in Judaism from separateness to moral purity, by the time of the New Testament (synchronic study) it meant largely moral purity while notions of separateness were only latent. Synchronic study is preferred over diachronic study for determining meaning because how a word developed and what it meant in the past may be of little value to the interpreter in understanding the particular time period under consideration.

The secret, if there is one, for doing responsible word studies is sensitivity to historical and authorial contexts. In failing to consider these two contexts, the interpreter will likely commit fundamental errors in determining meaning. One needs to pay attention to both paradigmatic and syntagmatic features, as well as diachronic developments and synchronic meanings.

Word Study Method

How does one do a word study in the Synoptics? To begin with, there are two basic steps (diachronic and synchronic) that are done with any word study. The goal of diachronic study is to trace the history of the meaning of a given term. After determining the etymology of a term, one needs to trace as fully as possible the historical development of that term in order to set the basic boundaries of its meaning at a specific time period. (A complete outline of how to accomplish such a task can be found in the introductory volume.) As this volume is concerned with the Synoptics, we need to look at the method of synchronic word analysis for the synoptic Gospels.

The major concern of the student of the Synoptics is the evidence of the Synoptics themselves and, in particular, of a single author (Mark, Matthew, Luke) because variations appear even between the Evangelists. The following procedure is recommended and a concordance to the Greek New Testament is absolutely essential. (There is only one complete concordance available.[1] Not

---

1. *Computer-Konkordanz zum Novum Testamentum Graece,* ed. by H. Bachmann and W. A. Slaby (Berlin and New York: Walter de Gruyter, 1980).

only are the lines long [thereby providing the reader with an imme-
diate grasp of the context], but the text is the standard Greek text of
the New Testament [Nestle-Aland, 26th ed.], unlike the Moulton
and Geden concordance, which is based on Westcott and Hort.[2])

Charting

The first step in doing a synchronic word analysis is to compose
a chart (see table 6). Write the word to be studied at the top of a
page. Next, locate the term in a concordance, and count the references. Then write out the number of the references in the Synoptics (or the particular author) in the left-hand vertical column.
Moving from left to right one should: (1) write down each reference; (2) tag the source (see "Tagging Words"); (3) record any
"formal" observations (see "Form"); (4) note the lexical meaning (or
the translation's term; see "Meaning"); and (5) record any connotations or observations (see "Connotations").

The student needs to recognize that each of these columns may
be vital in providing clues for determining meaning. At times the
frequency of a term in one Gospel is significant (e.g., σωτηρία in
Luke–Acts); at other times it may be the source; still other times it
may be significant to pay attention to "formal" elements. Most
often, however, it is the study of the contexts and observations on
usage patterns of each reference (connotations) that provide the
most important clues for determining meaning.

Tagging Words

The second step in doing a synchronic word analysis is to tag
each word. The purpose of this step is to identify, if possible, the
Gospel source of each word (see chap. 3). In recording a tag in the
source column, there are seven (and only seven) possibilities. And
though there may be different solutions to the Synoptic Problem,

---

2. For a discussion of the various concordances, see K. Aland, *The Text of the
New Testament* (Grand Rapids: Eerdmans, 1987), 263–66.

Table 6

Synoptic Synchronic Chart of πληρόω

	REFERENCE	SOURCE	FORM	MEANING	CONNOTATIONS
1	1:22	RM	πληρωθῇ	"Fulfill"	A pattern of Isaiah comes to pass in an event.
2	2:15	RM	πληρωθῇ	"Fulfill"	A pattern of Hosea etc.
3	2:17	RM	ἐπληρώθη	"Fulfill"	A pattern of Jeremiah etc.
4	2:23	RM	πληρωθῇ	"Fulfill"	A pattern of "the prophets" etc.
5	3:15	RM/RMk	πρέπον πληρῶσαι	"Fulfill"	To fulfill righteousness (all) by an act of baptism.
6	4:14	RMk	πληρωθῇ	"Fulfill"	A pattern of Isaiah comes to pass in an event.
7	5:17	RM	πληρῶσαι	"Fulfill"	Law and prophets are fulfilled in Jesus by? . . .
8	8:17	RMk	πληρωθῇ	"Fulfill"	A pattern of Isaiah comes to pass in Jesus' healing events.
9	12:17	RMk	πληρωθῇ	"Fulfill"	A pattern of Isaiah comes to pass in event of silencing.
10	13:35	RMk	πληρωθῇ	"Fulfill"	A pattern of Psalm 78:2 comes to pass in Jesus' parabolic teaching.
11	13:48	RM	ὅτε ἐπληρώθη	"Fill up a fishing net"	Filling a space.
12	21:4	RMk	πληρωθῇ	"Fulfill"	A pattern of Isaiah/Zechariah comes to pass in an event.

		RM/or RQ		"Fill up"	Command to complete the sins of one's ancestors.
13	23:32	RMk	πληρώσατε	"Fulfill"	How will OT prophecies (αἱ γραφαί) come to pass if resistance is used?
14	26:54	TMk	πληρωθῶσιν	"Fulfill"	Mtn R elements (adds τῶν προφητῶν) Event fulfills OT prophecies.
15	26:56	RM	πληρωθῶσιν	"Fulfill"	A pattern of Jeremiah comes to pass in an event.
16	27:9		ἐπληρώθη		

there remain only seven possibilities. (The following list assumes Markan priority and the existence of Q.) The possibilities are:

Mk: references to Mark when doing a word study in Mark

TMk: Matthew and/or Luke have taken a word from Mark

RMk: Matthew and/or Luke have added a word to Mark

TQ: Matthew and Luke have taken a word from Q

RQ: Matthew or Luke has added a word to Q

RM: Matthew alone has this word in what appears to be a tradition found only in Matthew

RL: Luke alone has this word in what appears to be a tradition found only in Luke

This is where underlining a synopsis will save time because one need only locate the word and observe its color in the synopsis. The following flow chart will enable the student to tag every word in a synopsis.

Mk

If the student is examining the meaning of a term in Mark, then every reference is tagged *Mk*. (Further study in the standard critical commentaries may convince the student that a given term may have been taken over by Mark from his sources.)[3]

TMk

If the student is examining Matthew or Luke:

If the story or saying is found in Matthew and/or Luke and in Mark (= a true parallel), and the word is found in Matthew and/or Luke and in Mark, then the tag is *TMk* (= a traditional word, i.e., Matthew and/or Luke have taken it from Mark). (Observe in Table 6 the fifteenth reference to πληρόω; this word is taken from Mark by Matthew.)

---

3. The issue of Markan style and redaction criticism is addressed in E. J. Pryke, *Redactional Style in the Marcan Gospel: A Study of Syntax and Vocabulary as Guides to Redaction in Mark*, Society for New Testament Studies Monograph Series, no. 33 (Cambridge: Cambridge University Press, 1978).

RMk

If the story or saying is found in Matthew and/or Luke and in Mark (= a true parallel), and the word is found in Matthew and/or Luke but not in Mark, then the tag is *RMk* (= a redactional word, i.e., Matthew and/or Luke have added it to Mark). (Observe the sixth, eighth, ninth, tenth, twelfth, fourteenth [and perhaps the fifth] reference to πληρόω in table 6; each of these records Matthew's addition to his Markan source.)

TQ

If the story or saying is found in Matthew and Luke but not in Mark, and the word is found in both Matthew and Luke, the word is tagged *TQ* (= a traditional word, i.e., both Matthew and Luke have taken it from Q). Since there are no references to "TQ" in table 6, one need only turn to Matthew 3:7 and Luke 3:7 and locate the term ὑπέδειξεν; this word would be tagged *TQ* since both Matthew and Luke have taken the term from their Q source.

RQ

If the story or saying is found in Matthew and Luke but not in Mark, and the word is not found in both Matthew and Luke, the word is tagged *RQ* (= a redactional word, i.e., either Matthew or Luke has added the word to the Q source). (It is possible that the thirteenth reference to πληρόω in table 6 has been added by Matthew to Q; it is also possible that it has come from Matthew's special source [see **RM**].)

RM or RL

If the story or saying is found only in Matthew or Luke, but with no parallel, the word is tagged *RM* (= found only in Matthew) or *RL* (= found only in Luke).[4] (Observe, in table 6, the first five references, which are all tagged *RM* because there is no true parallel to this word.)

---

4. Scholars also discuss whether RM or RL words were actually taken from the sources used by Matthew and Luke. In the case of πληρόω, in that the majority of references have been added by Matthew, it is reasonable to conclude that Matthew has added it at 3:15. Admittedly, one will fall short here of clear proof.

It is important to determine whether the word being examined is found in a passage with a true parallel. For example, in Matthew 3:13, the terms τότε, παραγίνεται, ἐπί, and πρός are tagged *RMk* since it appears that Matthew has added them to his Markan account. The terms Ἰησοῦς, ἀπό, Γαλιλαίας, and τὸν Ἰορδάνην should be tagged *TMk* since it appears that Matthew has conserved these from his Markan source. However, the term βαπτισθῆναι could be tagged *TQ* because it has a parallel in Luke (3:21) but, since this passage has a parallel in Mark and we are dealing with only one word, it should also be tagged *RMk* because it appears that Matthew and Luke both have added the term to their Markan source (Luke's use is tagged *RMk* as well). (In a synopsis, if one is looking at Matthew, blue and yellow indicate "TMk," red "TQ," and no color either "RMk," "RM," or "RQ." If one is looking at Luke, blue and green indicate "TMk," red "TQ," and no color either "RMk," "RL," or "RQ.")

This concern with "tags," however difficult to cope with at first, is not a pedantic one. It involves the ability of the exegete to trace the profile of how Matthew and Luke have used their sources. And, when it is possible to trace this profile and determine a clear pattern on the part of either author, some interesting features of Matthew's and Luke's theology begin to surface. Thus, tagging will often enable the serious exegete to find a sharper historical focus for determining meaning.

Source criticism will not resolve all problems for word studies in the Synoptics but it will sharpen the blade as the interpreter pierces through the pages of the synoptic Gospels. The goal of tagging is simple: to find patterns that exist in a particular Gospel (e.g., in Matthew—δικαιοσύνη, πληρόω, ἀναχωρέω, τῶν οὐρανῶν, μισθός; in Luke—δόξα, προσεύχομαι, πνεῦμα). Any student who investigates these words by means of tagging will gain a sharper historical profile and will be able to see lexical choice in action. Thus, one may reasonably argue that Matthew sees the term διδάσκαλος as one used by the enemies of Jesus in direct address whereas the disciples use κύριος; this stylistic feature motivates Matthew to use the contrasting terms in 8:19 and 8:21. Tagging helps one see this pattern at work.

On the one hand, tags are "scientifically objective" in that they are used to make word comparisons between the Synoptics; but, on the other, one cannot expect to find certainty in the matter.

Turning to Matthew 3:13–17 and its parallel in Luke 3:21–22, we observe that ambiguity exists, for example, around the term βαπτιοθῆναι. Did Matthew and Luke have a source in common? Or did they both coincidentally utilize this infinitive? Tagging may impute this to Q (Underlined in red) but that does not guarantee certainty on source-critical matters.

Form

The third step in doing a synchronic word analysis is to identify grammatical and syntactic form. The term *form* is intentionally ambiguous because it entails every possible feature of Greek grammar and syntax. On one occasion it may be the gender, another time case, and on yet another a combination of words. In doing research for my doctoral thesis, for example, I discovered that the preposition with βασιλεία in Matthew may be an important factor for determining the time to which the term refers (present or future kingdom?); and I concluded that the prepositions ἐν and εἰς betrayed futurity rather than realization. Such features are often quite suggestive for determining meaning.

Meaning

The fourth step is to ascertain the meaning of the word. The "Meaning" column is actually quite simple; in this column one fills in a rough "lexical meaning" of the Greek term being studied. This column will enable a quick overview of the various semantic ranges being used. (Observe in table 6 that only examples 11 and 13 are used in a way other than "fulfilling OT predictions.")

Connotations

The last step in doing a word study is to record any observations one might discover in studying the context of the term, taking note of associations with the particular word. In table 6 one will note that the notion of Old Testament prophecy regularly appears; one could also record the specific passage being fulfilled. This column is where most of the insights for meaning will appear; accordingly, there are no principles which can be given other than simply "observe" and "observe again."

When every reference in a particular Gospel has been examined, the student can study the entire chart for patterns and statistics—patterns between sources and forms, sources and connotations, forms and connotations, and so on. For example, the term ὑποκριτής in the Synoptics evinces some clear patterns. It occurs fourteen times in Matthew, one time in Mark, and three times in Luke. Of the fourteen occurrences in Matthew, only two, and perhaps three (7:5; 15:7; [cf. 22:18 with Mark 12:15]), came from Matthew's sources. Thus, the great majority were added, probably sometimes from M, to Matthew's Markan and Q sources (TMk: 1x; TQ: 1x; RMk: 1x; RQ: 5x; RM: 6x). Two features stand out: (1) the reason for the accusation varies significantly and cannot be restricted to "conscious pretense" as so many have argued (cf. 7:5; 22:18; 23:13, 15, 23, 29; 24:51); and (2) in Matthew, there is one group for whom this term is reserved, namely, the Pharisees. In Matthew 6:2, then, ὑποκριτής probably falls under the standard definition, "conscious pretense." Yet it also suggests that one of the reasons Jesus criticized this group for this practice is because they could lead others down their path of sin (see Matt. 23). Furthermore, in light of the great preponderance of uses referring to the Pharisees (see Matt. 23; 5:20), it is probable that Matthew has the Pharisees in mind here. Thus ὑποκριτής in this context means "the Pharisees who are consciously pretentious and who lead others in their path of pretense."

Word Statistics

Rarely are word statistics in the Synoptics determinative evidence; usually they are suggestive and confirmative evidence.[5]

5. Very few reference works have been concerned with the philosophical and mathematical issues involved when doing word statistics. A much criticized example is to be found in R. H. Gundry, *Matthew: A Commentary on His Literary and Theological Art* (Grand Rapids: Eerdmans, 1982). Though Gundry has not always

This can be seen in Matthew's use of πληρόω (see table 6). If one were to take all of the RM instances as from Matthew's sources (an approach which is possible; a decision either way cannot be determined with any probative force), the statistics would then be as follows: ten times from tradition and six times from redaction. If one reads the RM instances as redaction, the statistics would be as follows: one time from tradition, fifteen times from redaction. The difference is substantial and such disparity urges us to use extreme caution. However, several factors are vital.

Even if the RM instances are taken to be traditional, nevertheless Matthew has added them. Moreover, he has sixteen references whereas Mark has two or three and Luke nine. Furthermore, what one is examining is not percentage factors but "concentrations" of a given word in a given author and here Matthew rates "high." Consequently, what we are after is a pattern in a given author; and the pattern is there whether the terms come from his own hand or not. Thus, it is important to weigh the "statistics" against the patterns and theology to see if the statistics are significant. When a term is overwhelmingly preponderant in one Gospel (e.g., as εὐαγγελίζω is in Luke), then one has a vital clue for interpretation: such a term is one of a Gospel writer's favorites and the texts need to be examined for special nuances.

master a procedure which will permit solid conclusions. Not only should one pay attention to raw statistics (Matthew vs. Mark vs. Luke), but one also needs to note sources and forms. Word studies are basic for both the exegete and preacher of the Synoptics. Until the above procedure is mastered, the student will be handicapped as the exegesis process unfolds.

Which Words?

It is unfortunate that a word study of every word in a given passage is often held out as true expository preaching—unfortu-

---

used statistics carefully, his tables at the back are often helpful guides, and his work is exhaustive. A more sophisticated example is L. Gaston, *Horae Synopticae Electronicae: Word Statistics of the Synoptic Gospels,* Sources for Biblical Study, no. 3 (Missoula, Mont.: Society of Biblical Literature, 1973). An older, but painstakingly thorough, study is J. C. Hawkins, *Horae Synopticae,* 2d ed. (Oxford: Clarendon, 1908).

nate because no author in history has ever been that selective with words. Authors of the ancient world often chose words because of custom, style, and even in consideration of space (or lack thereof!). Students, then, need to learn to discern which words are significant for word study. There is no absolute rule. Choosing words is an art that requires prior experience. There are, however, a few guiding principles.

1. Words which are common theological terms throughout the Gospels need investigation. For example, one cannot deny that βασιλεία is an important term in the Gospels; it would, therefore, be irresponsible to preach from Mark 1:15 without having done a careful study of the term.
2. Terms which are favorites of an author deserve careful consideration. Students of Luke will want to investigate the term δόξα and students of Matthew δικαιοσύνη.
3. Words which, when altered in meaning, greatly affect the meaning of the passage at hand are important to study. An example is ὑποκριτής in Matthew 23 for, when one recognizes that the term includes such things as false understanding and false teaching, the meaning of the passage is drastically altered.[6]
4. Words which are ambiguous need to be studied, if only to keep the interpreter from attributing false ideas to them. As an example, though the meaning of μάγοι in Matthew 2:1 is not altogether clear, a solid study of the term will keep the interpreter from making the term mean things which it cannot mean.

These four principles should be kept in mind as the student seeks to determine which words are valuable for word analysis.

As mentioned previously, two elements of exegesis with special import for the Synoptics are word and motif analysis. Having looked at word studies, we now need to look at motif analysis.

---

6. I am indebted here to the excellent study of ὑποκριτής by D. E. Garland in *The Intention of Matthew 23*, Novum Testamentum Supplement 52 (Leiden: E. J. Brill, 1979), 96–123.

10

Motif Analysis

The term *motif* is used for a theological idea or theme which permeates an author's presentation. A motif is different from a word in that, whereas a word is restricted to one lexical unit, a motif encompasses associated words. Many have mistakenly identified the two and have done a motif analysis by means of a word study (e.g., investigating only ἀκολουθέω when actually intending to discover Matthew's *motif* of discipleship). If the word is sufficiently broad in meaning, a word study may accidentally result in a good motif study.

When does one do a motif study? After most of the steps of exegesis have been completed, a statement of an author's intention can be (and probably has been) roughly formed. The next step, and a crucial one, is to understand the passage within the compass of the broader ideas of the author.

Method

There is only one way to do a motif study: Read an entire Gospel for the purpose of obtaining all possible information from it relative to a given motif. As the student reads, he or she should note on paper every reference along with a brief description of how that verse or passage relates to that motif. It is usually the case that the Gospel will need to be read again, in that new categories emerge from the first reading. When the exegete is satisfied that all the data have been recorded and described, the major categories of the author, not categories drawn from either systematic theology or ecclesiastical questions, must be identified. The student should strive to be descriptive in the choice of terms when doing motif studies and biblical theology. After the major categories have been discovered, particular references need to be listed and then reexamined in order to define more precisely what is taught in that Gospel regarding that aspect of the motif.

Exemplar: Discipleship in Matthew

An adequate example of a motif study on discipleship in Matthew is included below.[1] One will notice immediately that this

---

1. For other studies on discipleship in Matthew, see G. Barth "Matthew's Understanding of the Law," in *Tradition and Interpretation in Matthew*, ed. by G. Bornkamm, G. Barth, and H. J. Held, 58–164 (Philadelphia: Westminster, 1963); G. Bornkamm, "End-Expectation and Church in Matthew," in *Tradition and Interpretation in Matthew*, ed. by G. Bornkamm, G. Barth, and H. J. Held, 15–51 (Philadelphia: Westminster, 1963); J. P. Burchill, "Discipleship Is Perfection," *Review for the Religious* 39 (1980): 36–42; W. D. Davies, *The Setting of the Sermon on the Mount* (Cambridge: Cambridge University Press, 1963); H. J. Held, "Matthew as Interpreter of the Miracle Stories," in *Tradition and Interpretation in Matthew*, ed. by G. Bornkamm, G. Barth, and H. J. Held, 165–299 (Philadelphia: Westminster, 1963); U. Luz, "The Disciples in the Gospel According to Matthew," in *The Interpretation of Matthew*, ed. by G. N. Stanton, 98–128 (Philadelphia: Fortress, 1983); R. Mohrlang, *Matthew and Paul: A Comparison of Perspectives*, Society for New Testament Study Monograph Series, no. 48 (Cambridge: Cambridge University Press, 1984); B. Przybylski, *Righteousness in Matthew and His World of Thought*, Society for New Testament Study Monograph Series, no. 41 (Cambridge: Cambridge University Press, 1980); L. Sabourin, *The Gospel According to St. Matthew* (Bandra, Bombay: St. Paul Publications, 1982), 109–24.

In addition to these specialized studies on Matthew, the following contain helpful discussions of Jesus' teaching on discipleship: D. Bonhoeffer, *The Cost of Discipleship* (New York: Macmillan, 1963); G. Bornkamm, *Jesus of Nazareth* (New York: Harper & Row, 1956); L. Goppelt, *Theology of the New Testament* (Grand Rapids: Eerdmans, 1981) 1:77–119; M. Hengel, *The Charismatic Leader and His Followers* (Edinburgh: T & T Clark, 1981); J. Jeremias, *New Testament Theology* (New York: Scribners, 1971); R. Schnackenburg, *The Moral Teaching of the New Testament* (New York: Seabury, 1962), 15–167; J. R. Martin, *Ventures in Discipleship: A Handbook for Groups or Individuals* (Scottdale, Penn.: Herald, 1984). The latter is an exemplary model for integrating exegesis, biblical theology, and historical theology with modern educational and discipling theories.

outline goes far beyond a word study, and that it could be developed even further by doing extensive word studies on various terms and an intensive exegesis of individual verses. Although it does not include critical debates (e.g., whether ἀπόστολος has Semitic or Greek roots), it does represent a basic outline of what Matthew means when he speaks of discipleship. The categories are natural; such notions as "church membership," "catechism," "relationship to pastoral authority," and the like, are not included.

Matthew 28:18–20

As a result of his vindication, Jesus has been given all authority (πᾶσα ἐξουσία; 18b) and, therefore, he gives his final direction to the disciples, here representing the church. The direction is "to make disciples" and this forms a logical place to begin our study.

The central command, and only finite verb, is "to disciple" (μαθητεύσατε), a command introduced apparently by a pleonastic participle. (The same form [the participle of πορεύομαι with an imperative] occurs in 2:8; 9:13; 10:7; 11:4; 17:27; 28:7.) In spite of this idiomatic usage of "going" (πορευθέντες), it should be noted that the same form (participle with imperative) is found several times in the LXX, and that the participle is usually a translation of a Hebrew Qal imperative (see Gen. 27:9, 13; 37:14; 43:2; Exod. 5:11, 18; 3 Kings 14:7; 4 Kings 5:10). Thus, the participle, though it does not have the same value in the sentence as the imperative, may well be more than a Semitic pleonasm.

The command to disciple all nations is further clarified by two participles (βαπτίζοντες, διδάσκοντες), yielding the following translation: "make disciples, that is to say, baptize and teach them." For those who are involved in this task, Jesus promises his presence (v. 20b; cf. 1:23).

Whereas the command to baptize clearly refers to the act whereby the convert publicly identifies with the Lord and the Lord's community, the term *teaching* is not so clear ("teaching them to keep whatever I have taught you"). This clause requires one to read the entire Gospel in order to understand what the teachings of Jesus are on discipleship. The clause also makes it clear that discipleship is demanded for all those who are part of the church. And so, we will now briefly survey the teachings in Matthew on discipleship.

The Call to Discipleship

A disciple is one who has been called by Jesus. In contrast to Jewish practice (the rabbinic student would volunteer to follow a certain rabbi after inspection of available rabbis), Jesus takes the initiative, acting with astounding authority in calling individuals to follow him (4:18–22; 9:9; 11:28–30; 15:13; 19:21; 28:18–20); he also discourages superficial volunteers (8:18–22; 19:16–22). Those called: (1) have faith (8:10, 13, 23–27; 9:2, 22, 28–29; 13:58; 15:28; 17:20; 21:21–22, 32); (2) receive the forgiveness of sins (9:2–8, 10–13); and (3) receive the revelation of God's mysteries (11:25–27; 13:1–52, esp. vv. 10–17, 23, 34–35, 51–52; 16:12, 17–20, 21; 17:1–13, 22–23; 20:17–19; 24:1–25:46; 26:2).

Tasks of the Disciple

Disciples are called to: (1) proclaim the gospel, pronounce judgment, and participate in the ministry of Jesus (4:18–22; 10:5–8, 13–15; 16:19; 18:17–18; 24:14; 26:13; 28:18–20); (2) influence the world around them (5:13–16); (3) experience table fellowship and communion with Jesus (9:9–13; 10:8–13, 40–42; 12:46–50; 16:18; 18:5, 18, 19–20; 20:1–16; 21:43; 22:8–12; 25:31–46; 26:17–30), a fellowship rooted in brotherhood (20:1–16; 23:8–12) and mutual service (20:24–28; 23:11); (4) perform the ministry of Jesus (cf. 8:1–9:34 with 9:35–11:1; 10:5–6 with 15:24); (5) teach the doctrines of Jesus (5:19; 13:51–52; 23:8–10; 28:20); and (6) worship and confess Jesus (10:32–33; 14:33; 16:16).

Terms for the Disciple

In Matthew, disciples are portrayed as fishermen (4:19), followers (4:18–22; 8:18–22; 19:21), students (5:1–7:29; 9:35–11:1; 13:1–52; 18:1–19:1; 23:1–39; 23:1–26:1), salt (5:13), light (5:14–16), scribes (13:51–52), and servants (20:24–28). (Other portraits can be found by sifting through Matthew's vocabulary; these can be explored for the light they shed on the nature of discipleship.)

Demands of the Disciple

For those who decide to follow Jesus, great demands are made; Jesus despises superficial, idolatrous commitments. Disciples must have no higher priority, whether that be family, job, wealth, or life itself (4:18–22; 6:25–34; 8:21–22; 9:9; 10:21–22, 34–39); and must expect to share the fate of the prophets, John the Baptist, and Jesus (10:24–25; 16:24–28; 5:10–12; 8:18–20; 10:16–39; 11:12; 17:11–12; 20:22–23; 23:34–36; 24:9; 27:57–75). Because these demands result in rejection, disciples are few in number (7:13–14, 21–23; 13:1–9, 18–23; 18:6–9; 19:30; 20:16; 22:11–14; 24:10–13; 25:31–46; 26:21–25, 31–35).

Being a disciple of Jesus entails the loss of security: vocational (4:18–22; 9:9), familial (4:18–22; 10:21, 34–39; 12:46–50), financial (4:18–22; 6:25–34; 19:16–26), physical (10:17–23, 38; 16:24–28; 23:34–36), religious (8:21–22), social (5:11–12; 10:22, 24–25), and personal (16:24–28).

Characteristics of the Disciple

What are the traits of a disciple of Jesus? How does Jesus, in his teachings in Matthew, describe the "virtuous life" of one of his followers? To answer this question is to delve into an aspect of the teaching of Jesus which is well-nigh endless. The following list is representative.

1. Humility (5:3; 6:12, 13; 16:24–27; 18:1–5; 23:12)
2. Righteousness (5:6, 8, 10, 14–16, 19, 20, 21–48; 6:1–18; 7:15–27; 9:17; 12:1–8, 33–37, 48–50; 13:1–9, 18–23, 41, 43, 49; 15:1–20; 19:2–12, esp. vv. 9–12; 21:28–32; 24:45–51; 25:14–30; 28:20)
3. Forgiving spirit (5:7, 23–26; 6:12, 14–15; 18:15–20, 21–35)
4. Peacefulness (5:9, 38–42; 13:24–30, 36–43; 17:24–27; 22:15–22; 26:50–54)
5. Nonhypocrisy (5:20; 6:1, 2–18; 7:1–5; 22:18; 23:1–36; 24:51)
6. Honesty (5:33–37)
7. Daily trust (6:11, 25–34; 8:20; 10:8–10, 19–20, 26–33)
8. Seeking the kingdom (6:10, 19–34)
9. Nonmaterialism (4:18–22; 6:19–34; 13:22; 19:23–30)
10. Nonjudgmental attitudes (7:1)
11. Respect for sacred things (7:6; 10:16, 23)
12. Perseverance (10:22, 32–33, 38; 13:20–21; 24:13)
13. Fearlessness (10:26–33; 14:27)
14. Compassion (9:12–13; 12:7; 18:10–14)

15. Watchfulness (24:36–25:46; 26:38, 41)

Three terms that summarize these virtues in Matthew are love
(5:43–47; 7:12; 22:34–40; 23:23), perfection (wholeness of response;
5:48; 6:22–24; 8:19, 22; 10:39; 13:44–46; 19:16–22, 27–30) and righteousness (3:15; 5:6, 10, 20; 6:1, 33; 21:32).

Failure in Discipleship

In spite of these demands and characteristics, Jesus does not
demand sinless perfection of the disciple. In fact, throughout the
Gospels (especially in Mark), the disciple of Jesus fails in discipleship. There are at least two basic reasons for this failure: "little
faith" (ὀλιγοπιστία; 8:23–27; 14:22–33; 16:8; 17:14–21) and a lack of
understanding (14:15–21; 15:15–20, 23, 33; 16:9–11, 21–23; 17:4, 10,
23; 18:1, 21; 19:13, 25; 20:24–28; 21:20; 26:8–13; 28:17). (One should
not be led to the inference that every failure is to be classed under
one of these two headings.)

The Unlikely

A distinctive emphasis of the Gospels is the surprising composition of the disciple band. Contrary to Jewish expectations, Jesus
ministered to the unlikely, that is, to those who were not expected
to be the "in" group. These people are often paradigms of percep-
tion and faith, not to mention "grace," in the Gospels. Thus, lepers
(8:2–4), gentile centurions (8:5–13; 27:54), women (8:14–15; 9:20–22;
15:21–28; 26:6–13; 27:55–56; 28:1–10), the demon-possessed (8:16–
17, 28–34; 9:32–34; 12:22–24), paralytics (9:1–8), the blind (9:27–31;
20:29–34), the dumb (9:32–34), unlearned (11:25–27), gentile
women (15:21–28), children (18:1–9; 19:13–15), tax collectors
(9:9–13; 21:32) and prostitutes (21:28–32), as well as Joseph of
Arimathea (27:57–61), respond when the more "likely" (Pharisees,
scribes, Sadducees) do not.

Promises for Disciples

The disciple of Jesus is promised, for the present, physical provisions (6:33; 19:29), spiritual rest (11:29), and Jesus' continual pres-

ence (28:20) and, for the future, the Father's approbation (6:1, 4, 6, 18; 10:40–42; 16:27; 20:1–16), acquittal (12:37), the kingdom of heaven (5:3–12), rule over others (19:28), eternal life (19:29), and eternal table fellowship at the Father's feast (8:11–12; 26:27–29).

Motif studies are important for the student and pastor since it is at this level that the passage in a particular Gospel is placed in its proper context—and we are all too well aware of passages being mistreated and misapplied due to interpretation apart from the author's context.

The student, if doing a study of a passage in Matthew (this may apply to Mark and Luke as well) which touches upon discipleship (e.g., Matt. 4:18–22), would need to understand this passage in light of the above survey. Understanding passages in their larger contexts has manifold implications. For example, since discipleship involves a life-style of obedience and righteousness, the call to follow Jesus in 4:18–22 is not exclusively a call to evangelism but also a call to walk righteously.

Matthew 6:33 promises physical provisions to the followers of Jesus. This verse, however, is often interpreted in such a way to lead people to think that God will give them anything they de-sire—from computers to oil fields! But, in the context of Matthew, there are no promises of luxury—only the assurance that God will look after his own by providing their daily needs (see Matt. 6:9–13). Accordingly, Matthew 6:33 is misapplied when one infers that Jesus is guaranteeing "health, wealth, and prosperity." The exegete who desires to be accurate asks, "To what could ταῦτα refer in the *context* of Matthew's Gospel?" not, "To what could I apply this in order to get what I want?"

Bibliography for Motif Analysis

Since the standard word books of the New Testament have not stuck to their task (words) and have instead often done motif stud-ies, the student will sometimes find valuable discussions of motifs there (see G. Kittel and C. Brown). After personal study of a given motif, the student will do well to consult these books to see if any valuable ideas have been omitted or data overlooked. Furthermore, many of the finer commentaries have extensive discussions on the "theology" of Matthew, Mark, or Luke. One need only consult the excellent introductions of L. Sabourin (Matthew), W. L. Lane (Mark), and J. A. Fitzmyer (Luke) to see how inviting motif studies are for the Synoptics.

The final extension of motif study involves comparing the teaching of a given author with other authors of the New Testament and, ultimately, the entire canon—a process known as "biblical theology." At this point the student will almost always have to rely upon the standard New Testament theologies to complete the task since time usually prohibits one from doing a complete biblical theology of a topic. And this part of the task needs to be extended by comparing the results with "systematic theology." To do this, the student will need to compare his or her idea with the appropriate sections in a systematic theology. For example, for discipleship in Matthew one might examine the "Lordship of Christ" in a Christology section, the "Christian Life" in another section, and perhaps "Sanctification" under the Holy Spirit. It is absolutely imperative that a student compare results in light of systematic theology—if only to prevent errors. Systematic theology should not determine conclusions in exegesis; rather, exegesis challenges systematic formulations. However, the student should pause long and hard before venturing to disagree with orthodoxy.

The Teachings of Jesus

A related, but separate, form of motif study is the examination of the teachings of Jesus throughout all four Gospels.[2] Such examination is related because it is motif analysis, intended to compose a complete theology of Jesus. It is separate, however, because it is not restricted to one Gospel; further, the minute one begins to work on the "teachings of Jesus" one also faces questions pertaining to historical reliability. The procedures are different in that examination of the teachings of Jesus takes into consideration all four Gospels

---

2. See Jeremias, *New Testament Theology;* R. H. Stein, *The Method and Message of Jesus' Teachings* (Philadelphia: Westminster, 1978); Goppelt, *Theology of the New Testament.*

rather than just one. Furthermore, in doing motif analysis one will want to consider redactional emphases as well as literary strategies paramount; on the other hand, in doing "teaching of Jesus" studies, the approach is much more "harmonistic."

Conclusion

In conclusion, we shall summarize the method of synoptic exegesis.

First, the student needs to come to some intelligent conclusions about introductory questions pertaining to authorship, provenance, structure, and the *Sitz im Leben* out of which a synoptic Gospel grew. Further, every student of the Synoptics needs to study, in as great detail as possible, the original texts as well as the major secondary treatments of the history, social conditions, and religious practices and beliefs of the ancient world. In addition, the student needs to work carefully through a synopsis in order to frame an intelligent conclusion regarding the relationship of the synoptic Gospels.

After these preliminary matters have been settled (and the student will inevitably accomplish this during study of the Gospels themselves), the following procedures in exegeting a synoptic Gospel need to be performed:

1. Having roughly translated a pericope, the text of that pericope needs to be established and the apparatus should be read carefully.
2. The grammatical and syntactical features of the pericope ought to be thoroughly examined.
3. The insights of the tradition-critical methods need to be applied to that pericope (tradition, form, redaction, and literary criticism).
4. During this time the student must thoroughly examine the profile an author gives to particular words in the pericope.

119

5. When analysis of the passage has been completed, the student will want to expand a theological understanding of the author's intention by accomplishing motif analysis of the major themes and ideas of the pericope.

6. The exegetical process concludes with a final translation of the pericope and a succinct statement of the author's intention.

It is my hope that this guide to synoptic exegesis will encourage many students to study the synoptic Gospels and aid them in their pursuit of the authors' intended meanings. It is my greatest hope, however, that the Lord of the synoptic Gospels will be experienced more deeply and known more completely through this book.

Appendix

Literary Criticism

The most recent development in Gospel studies, growing out of the interaction of biblical studies with the liberal arts, is literary criticism; it is the purpose of this appendix to explain and evaluate its usefulness for understanding the meaning of the synoptic Gospels. Before defining *literary criticism*, several introductory comments are in order.

Literary criticism is a predictable child of redaction criticism, for in literary criticism one finds a consistent and embracing concern with the text as it is.[1] If redaction criticism censures form and source criticism's preoccupation with stages *prior* to the text, then literary criticism consummates that concern. Yet such a "birth" is not altogether natural because, whereas redaction criticism is a development of the tradition-critical process, literary criticism is not. Thus, although the concerns of redaction criticism (in its compositional aspects) and those of literary criticism (the meaning of the final text) are often similar, their heritages are so dissimilar that one must recognize a paradigmatic revolution in literary criticism. If redaction criticism emerged from the historical-critical concerns of Gospel scholarship, literary criticism emerged from *anti*historical-

---

1. For recent studies on the origins of literary criticism in biblical studies, see N. R. Petersen, *Literary Criticism for New Testament Critics* (Philadelphia: Fortress, 1978), 9–23; R. Alter, *The Art of Biblical Narrative* (New York: Basic Books, 1981), 3–22.

critical forces and the theoretical analysis of nonbiblical literature, particularly the examination of prose fiction.

One may be led by the preceding paragraph to think "literary criticism" is a unified, singular approach (even school) in Gospel studies but this is simply not the case. In fact, the approaches often classed under the term *literary criticism* are quite diverse, including such methods as structuralism, rhetorical criticism, narrative criticism, canon criticism, reader-response criticism, and even deconstructionism—each with its own history, concerns, methods, evangelists, administrative assistants, and (most especially) jargon. This appendix concerns primarily narrative criticism.

This means that when we look at Gospel literary critics for the purpose of defining the discipline, we observe what Gospel literary critics are doing (description) and not what they must do (prescription).[2] There is no such thing as *the* literary approach to the Gospels. Consequently, students should read further in the works cited.

Definition and Explanation

Literary criticism is a discipline of literary critics which seeks, by literary analysis, to explain a text as a vehicle of communication between an author and audience.

First, literary criticism has a self-conscious stance over against the traditional historical-critical method. One need not read very far in most literary critics before they are evangelistically contrasting a "literary reading" of the text at hand with a "historical

---

2. There is not yet a full-scale "poetics of gospel narrative." The most complete and accurate studies of biblical literary criticism to date are M. Sternberg, *The Poetics of Biblical Narrative: Ideological Literature and the Drama of Reading*, Indiana Literary Biblical Series (Bloomington: Indiana University Press, 1985); Alter, *Biblical Narrative*; Petersen, *Literary Criticism*. For the application of literary theory to the Gospels, see D. Rhoads and D. Michie, *Mark as Story: An Introduction to the Narrative of a Gospel* (Philadelphia: Fortress, 1982); J. D. Kingsbury, *Matthew as Story* (Philadelphia: Fortress, 1986); R. C. Tannehill, *The Narrative Unity of Luke-Acts: A Literary Interpretation* (Philadelphia: Fortress, 1986).

reading" of the same text.[3] Freighted expressions like "excavative scholarship," "text versus event," "evolutionary models," "referential fallacy," "intrinsic versus extrinsic approach," and "geneticism" appear frequently to maintain the methodological distinction between looking *through* the text and looking *at* the text. M. Sternberg, however, warns: "But they [those doing literary analyses] must soon reach a point of diminishing returns unless they spend less energy on self-assertion vis-à-vis traditional scholarship and more on a systematic examination of their own aims and equipment."[4]

Second, literary criticism is usually either ahistorical or antihistorical in its interpretative practice. In emphasizing a "nonreferential reading" of a text, literary critics are often self-consciously ambivalent about, or even resistant to, the origins, evolution, setting, and referents of the text and, at times, the intention of the author. This point must be presented carefully because literary critics differ on the value of background information and historical referents. Some deny altogether that the goal of exegesis (interpretation) is to discover the author's intention, describing such a goal as an "intentional fallacy." Others speak of the "autonomous nature" of the text, "authorial irrelevance," or an "antihistoricistic approach." Still others resist any interpretations apart from author's intention in its context but still proceed in what may be called an "ahistorical" manner, that is, rarely is their concern with Luke's *Sitz im Leben* or the historical reliability of a given saying of Jesus.[5]

However, such a stance is not a *necessary* depreciation of the reliability of the events. Instead, such scholars conclude that whether or not an event happened plays no role in interpreting the

---

3. H. Frei has done the most for driving a wedge between historical referentiality (looking through a text at its referent) and literary analysis. See esp. *The Eclipse of Biblical Narrative: A Study in Eighteenth and Nineteenth Century Hermeneutics* (New Haven, Conn.: Yale University Press, 1974). For a succinct criticism of the historical-critical method and defense of the literary approach, see R. A. Culpepper, "Story and History in the Gospels," *Review & Expositor* 81 (1984): 467–78.

4. Sternberg, *Poetics*, 56.

5. See E. D. Hirsch, Jr., *Validity in Interpretation* (New Haven, Conn.: Yale University Press, 1967), 1–23; Petersen, *Literary Criticism*, 24–48; Sternberg, *Poetics*, 8–9. For a defense of a fictional understanding of the Bible, see J. C. Collins, "The Rediscovery of Biblical Narrative," *Chicago Studies* 21 (1982): 45–58.

text. R. A. Culpepper argues that "if the gospels depict primarily neither the actual history of Jesus' ministry nor the situation in which they were written but a narrative world, and if the meaning of the gospel narratives lies on this side of the text and requires the response of the reader, then the extent to which the gospels accurately represent the ministry of Jesus is irrelevant for understanding their meaning."[6]

Third, literary critics emphasize the literary nature of the author. If redaction criticism returns to the author, then literary criticism has become preoccupied with the author—sometimes to the point of identifying the author with the text. And the author is explained in very sophisticated categories. Thus, some literary critics distinguish between the "real author" (say, Mark himself), the "implied author" (the literary version of Mark as discerned from the text), and the "narrator" (Mark's voice in the narrative or the one whom we hear as we read the text, i.e., in rough terms, the "black letters" in the red-letter edition Bibles). In spite of this careful delineation, most literary theorists who work in biblical literature do not make distinctions between the implied author and the narrator; there is, however, a distinction between this narrator and the historical personage who penned the individual Gospel.

In a way which seems to uncover some of the mystery of inspiration, literary critics speak of the omniscience, omnicompetence, and omnipresence of the narrator (not the real author).[7] Certainly those who are familiar with biblical narratives recognize that the narrators of the texts, in their third-person reports, seem to be privy to hidden motives (even God's), secret schemes, and psychological developments. Yet the narrator never explains his accessibility to such information. We have then a self-effacing author (one who never presents himself) who seems to know everything (omniscience). Further, he regularly lets his readers in on this information so that they know more about the truth than the characters. One thinks here of the disciples in Mark, as they fumble through life trying to figure out just who Jesus is. All the while Mark knows

---

6. Culpepper, "Story and History," 473.

7. See Sternberg, *Poetics*, 84–128; Alter, *Biblical Narrative*, 155–57; S. Chatman, *Story and Discourse: Narrative Structure in Fiction and Film* (Ithaca, N.Y.: Cornell University Press, 1978), 146–62; Kingsbury, *Matthew*, 29–32; Rhoads and Michie, *Mark*, 35–43.

the answers and has told his readers (see Mark 1:1). As the disciples stumble along, the readers groan in anticipation of the disciples' discovery, knowing all the time just who Jesus is.

The narrator is also omnicompetent in that he has the capacity to order and arrange, to predict an event and then bring it into fulfillment, and to manipulate and control his facts and events to bring them into the order he chooses for the purposes he desires. The narrator has the capability at times to step into the picture and tell his readers some information (Matthew tells us, for instance, that Judas betrayed Jesus well before the arrest [10:4]), or he can cause ambiguity and gaps in our knowledge by withholding such desired information (Matthew does not tell us whether Peter will return after the predicted denial [26:35]; this creates suspense and curiosity).

A final element of this literary nature of the author is his omnipresence. As an invisible participant in the events of the narrative and discourses, the narrator hovers over everything, seeing an action here, hiding an event there, and reporting to his readers the results. Thus, Luke (as narrator) is "present" at the birth of John and Jesus (1–2), overhears Herod's musings about John (9:7–9), and watches the resurrection appearances (24).

Fourth, though literary critics often express the manifold nature of a text (historical impulse, ideological orientation, and aesthetic form), they are preeminently concerned with the literary, or aesthetic, nature of the text as a work of literature. Thus, these critics are concerned with the nature of linear sequence, plot, geographical movement, and literary devices.[8] Literary critics are interested in the formal nature of the text, its relationship, say, to Greek tragedy, to Philostratus's *Life of Apollonius of Tyana*, or even to nineteenth-century French and English prose fiction.

Integral to the literary critic's understanding of the text as literature is a concern with the unity of the text (especially in the face of tradition criticism's sporadic accusations of the Evangelists' clum-

---

8. For a discussion of the various devices that literary theorists perceive in biblical narratives, see C. H. Lohr, "Oral Techniques in the Gospel of Matthew," *Catholic Biblical Quarterly* 23 (1961): 403–35; V. K. Robbins, *Jesus the Teacher: A Socio-Rhetorical Interpretation of Mark* (Philadelphia: Fortress, 1984), 1–73; Sternberg, *Poetics*, 35–41; Rhoads and Michie, *Mark*, 45–62; Petersen, *Literary Criticism*, 49–92.

siness in passing on traditions). For example, rather than seeing a bungling combination of disparate traditions, literary critics want to know why Matthew has utilized both Matthew 10:5–6 and 28:16–20 in the same Gospel. R. C. Tannehill sees God's purpose of salvation for mankind as that which unifies the narrative of Luke–Acts in spite of the tension created by rejection.[9] For the literary critic, the unity of the text is a necessary presupposition.

Further, the narrator uses characters, settings, and events to produce the story line and so effect the desired response from his readers. One of the integral facets of literary theory is that a text is interpreted by seeing what the author does in the text with elements of that text. The narrator of Matthew paints the picture of the Pharisees black and colors Jesus brightly in order to demonstrate to his readers that Jesus is the Messiah while the ways of the Pharisees and scribes is the way of death.

Fifth, literary critics are concerned with a text as a vehicle of communication and how the reader construes meaning through it. Again, as with the author, literary theorists operate with a sophisticated analysis of the reader. Thus, some divide reader into the "real reader" (any human, ancient or modern, who reads the text), the "implied reader" (the imaginary person who responds appropriately to each of the narrator's strategies), and the "narratee" (the specific audience of the narrator's direct comments). But again, besides the bewildering confusion which can arise from such distinctions, few biblical literary theorists operate with such distinctions; instead, the reader is usually considered to be the implied reader.

Reader-oriented criticism is much less concerned with what a text means and much more with what a text does to the reader.[10] For reader-response critics, in order for a text to have meaning a reader must necessarily be active, interacting with the expectations forced on him or her through the text as those expectations work toward fulfillment or disappointment. Thus, readers make assumptions and revise those assumptions, they conclude and then

---

9. See *Narrative Unity*.

10. See R. M. Fowler, "Who Is the 'Reader' of Mark's Gospel?," *Society of Biblical Literature Seminar Papers* (1983): 31–54; J. L. Resseguie, "Reader-Response Criticism and the Synoptic Gospels," *Journal of the American Academy of Religion* 52 (1984): 307–24; Kingsbury, *Matthew*, 36–38.

reformulate those conclusions through unexpected textual patterns, and they ask questions and await answers to those questions from the text.

These are some of the main features which confront the student of literary criticism in Gospel studies. Literary criticism has made an important contribution to our understanding of the Gospels, but it has not become an "established method," nor has it refined its own methodology so as to present a "poetics of Gospel narrative." Even a dim-sighted seer sees fuller treatments ahead. In the following sections I shall offer some criticisms of the discipline as practiced and then make further suggestions as to its value for Gospel research.

Negative Evaluation of Literary Criticism

The following criticisms do not apply in the same degree to each literary theorist. The criticisms are directed toward those weaknesses and inaccurate principles which students must avoid as they attempt to grapple with the literary nature of the Gospel narratives.

The most obvious weakness is literary criticism's depreciation of the importance of the real author's intent, historical reference, and background information for understanding texts. Not all scholars disparage the real author or background information, but most regard authorship, date, provenance, and audience as "interesting irrelevancies." This problem, of course, relates directly to the self-conscious, ahistorical approach of much of literary criticism. The questions which need to be raised are these: Were the Gospel authors referentially oriented and concerned? Do the events and sayings themselves have any relevance to, or any restrictive determinations for, the author as he composes his text? Did Mark utilize the call of the disciples when he did because it happened that way or because of a literary convention? Does the author conceive of himself as writing history, writing literature, or both? In other words, as a Gospel author sat down to write, was he writing to describe what took place and what was said, or was he simply attempting to persuade his audience through a literary strategy? The answers to these highly important questions have manifold ramifications for interpretation. Consequently, there needs to be serious research by scholars into the issue of referentiality and nonreferentiality in the ancient world.

A recent brilliant essay on American education by E. D. Hirsch, Jr., is illuminating at this point.[11] Hirsch's concern is with decreasing levels of "cultural literacy," the "network of information that all competent readers possess" in American education and society.[12] In detailing not only the problem but also a solution, Hirsch writes indirectly about the importance of background information for any form of communication even to take place.

Hirsch notes:

> The recently rediscovered insight that literacy is more than a skill is based upon knowledge that all of us unconsciously have about language. We know instinctively that to understand what somebody is saying, we must understand more than the surface meanings of words; we have to understand the context as well. The need for background information applies all the more to reading and writing. To grasp the words on a page we have to know a lot of information that isn't set down on the page.[13]

In citing advancing scholarship in the nature of reading and learning, Hirsch clearly demonstrates that background is not only important; in fact, schemata of previously acquired information are what separates those who understand from those who do not.[14] Literary theorists may stand in awe of the ice "floating on" the water. They may describe its aesthetic shape and its evocative powers, but sooner or later their ship will awaken to a crashing "Titanic-like" revelation of the fact that what they were staring at was in fact an iceberg, with much more below the surface than above. So whether we are after the meaning of a Hebrew term in Psalms or a cultural practice in the Gospels, it is absolutely imperative that we dig behind the text to find out information which might shed light on the text as it is.

To continue to propagate the notion of an autonomous text, which is not anchored in a real author and a real audience, is

---

11. *Cultural Literacy: What Every American Needs to Know* (Boston: Houghton Mifflin, 1987).

12. Ibid., 2.

13. Ibid., 3.

14. Ibid., esp. 33–69.

methodologically unjustified. Such a postulate is no longer accepted by literary critics at large and should be abandoned by biblical literary theorists as well. Sternberg argues that "the text's autonomy is a long-exploded myth: the text has no meaning, or may assume every kind of meaning, outside those coordinates of discourse that we usually bundle into the term 'context.'"[15]

One example from the Gospels can aid this discussion pertaining to background. In Mark 13:14 we read an intentional, intruding comment by the author: "let the reader understand." The author is consciously aware that his readers are a literary guild but, more importantly, what he has spoken in oblique, intentionally ambiguous language is consciously referring to extratextual factors which the reader is supposed to decode in order to understand the meaning of the text itself. This means that at least some of Mark is referentially oriented (he is referring to things); if this is so, some of Mark will simply not be understood unless one understands the referents themselves. To grasp Mark's intention we must examine background information about the "abomination of desolation," about Mark's setting, and about Jesus' teachings.

In larger terms, this entire discussion on the value of events and referentiality is related to biblical theology as the unfolding of the acts of God for people and the consequent scriptural revelation (a deed-word revelation).[16] In spite of literary criticism's dismissal of *Heilsgeschichte*, two issues remain: (1) the New Testament authors consistently categorize theology in salvation-historical terms without reference to authors and literary patterns (e.g., Acts 7:2–53; Gal. 3:19–25; 4:4–5); and (2) there is a stubborn commitment to the importance of facts and referentiality in a broad spectrum of New Testament scholarship.

In conclusion, until literary theorists can prove that the Gospels have little or no referential orientation, it is unlikely that they will

---

15. Sternberg, *Poetics*, 11.

16. An excellent anthology of essays dealing with the importance of historical reliability and events for truth, exegesis, and New Testament theology is C. F. H. Henry, ed., *Jesus of Nazareth: Saviour and Lord* (Grand Rapids: Eerdmans, 1966; esp. K. S. Kantzer, "The Christ-Revelation as Act and Interpretation," 243–64); see also G. E. Ladd, *A Theology of the New Testament* (Grand Rapids: Eerdmans, 1974), 13–33; E. Hoskyns and N. Davey, *The Riddle of the New Testament* (London: Faber & Faber, 1947).

convince the scholarly guild of the sufficiency of their approach and, more importantly, they will not yield accurate understandings of the authors' intentions as made known in and through the individual Gospels.

A second weakness of the approach of the literary critics is that their reading, which is claimed by H. Frei to be precritical, is at odds with the readings we have from the earliest churches. Not only is there a clear historical consciousness in the New Testament itself, but the results of redaction criticism and the earliest commentaries on the Gospels, especially Augustine's (see *Harmony* 1:1–2, 7; passim), show marked interest in ostensive reference and in the historical Jesus. In fact, it can be said that the early church largely understood the Gospels as reports about the historical Jesus, what he did, and what he said. Apart from some general comments which lead in a redaction-critical direction in authors like Augustine (*Harmony* 1:2–6), there are no early church writings which treat the Gospels as literary masterpieces, nor extensive comments which prove that the interpreters were interested in such things as plot, technique, character development, and the like. This may simply prove that the earliest churches completely failed to understand the literary shaping by the original authors, but this is doubtful. Until there is some unambiguous evidence to bolster such a literary consciousness on the part of the early church, we would do well to hold literary criticism in check by what appears to be a consistent, referential reading by the earliest churches. Instead of looking to H. S. Reimarus and R. Simon, perhaps we might look to Mark, Q, Matthew, Luke, and John for the origin of the quest for the historical Jesus.

A third criticism is the potentially misleading method of comparing the Gospels with modern fiction. In spite of the claim by both Sternberg and Alter to fashion a truly "biblical poetics" which, only after inductive demonstration, is compared with modern literature (hence, the constant analogies with Dickens, Fielding, Henry James, and so on), too much of literary criticism is rooted in genre analysis of modern fiction. Whether it is character analysis, understandings of author, text, and readers, or plot, too often those who are concerned with the literary nature of the Gospels establish their categories from modern literature. A notable and refreshing exception to this rule is the work of V. K. Robbins, who attempts to understand the genre of the Gospels on the basis of ancient Jewish and Graeco-Roman conventions.[17] It should be noted that comparison with modern fiction is not necessarily improper; our criticism has to do with which work of literature has priority in setting the categories.[18]

A fourth criticism pertains to the method of fashioning an appropriate exegetical model. Literary criticism consciously and methodologically avoids examining the tradition-critical process in seeking to determine the meaning of the text. Yet, can any method which studiously avoids facts about how the text came into existence be accurate? In other words, though scholars are not agreed as to the order of the Gospels, they are in virtual agreement that the Gospels are interdependent. If there is a relationship, is it not methodologically naive and intentionally blind to avoid such data in framing a method?

Accordingly, it is methodologically erroneous to read Matthew and Luke without looking at Mark to see what the other two Evangelists have done to Mark in drafting their Gospels. N. R. Petersen accurately observes: "But while Mark was not a completely free narrator, redaction critics have made it equally clear that he was not completely dependent either."[19] The fact is that if the Gospels are interdependent, then a method which purposefully ignores such interdependence is doomed to inaccuracy. And yet literary criticism has not avoided this problem. In fact, R. C. Tannehill can, after contending that he accepts the Oxford Hypothesis, assert that "this view does not affect [the] following interpretations."[20]

---

17. See *Jesus the Teacher*. While Robbins's strength is his anchoring of the Gospel genre in ancient genres, his weakness is his unwillingness to grant significant development on the part of the Gospel authors.

18. See R. A. Guelich, "The Gospel Genre," in *Das Evangelium und die Evangelien: Vorträge vom Tübinger Symposium 1982*, Wissenschaftliche Untersuchungen zum Neuen Testament, no. 28 (Tübingen: J. C. B. Mohr [Paul Siebeck], 1983), 183–219; R. H. Gundry, "Recent Investigations into the Literary Genre 'Gospel,'" in *New Dimensions in New Testament Study*, ed. by R. N. Longenecker and M. C. Tenney, 97–114 (Grand Rapids: Zondervan, 1974). Comparison has led some scholars to contend that the Gospels are *sui generis*; for an attempt to urge them to think more comparatively, see L. Ryken, "Literary Criticism of the Bible: Some Fallacies," in *Literary Interpretations of Biblical Narratives*, ed. by K. R. R. Gros Luis, et al., 24–40, esp. 30–33 (Nashville: Abingdon, 1974).

19. Petersen, *Literary Criticism*, 23, 24.

20. Tannehill, *Narrative Unity*, 6 n. 3.

Thus, the debate cannot be reduced to a simple "this is my procedure and that is your approach—perhaps we shall illuminate one another and the text." The issue more accurately concerns which method most corresponds to the data in the text itself.

Fifth, a minor problem with literary criticism is a preoccupation with literary techniques which occasionally leads to "parallelomania" or finding such techniques at work which are far from obvious. It is not necessary to belabor this point simply because it is a matter of excess and not of substance. The problem is seen when scholars insist on finding chiasms, when every geographical reference is forced into a literary allusion, when one wrings a pattern of "threes" or "fives" from the text, or when character development is found and the text simply does not yield such a reading naturally.

A sixth problem is that occasionally literary (especially reader-oriented) critics forget that the readers of this literature are not learning about Jesus for the first time. Too frequently one finds an approach to reading the Gospels which sounds too much like a "tabula rasa" orientation in which the reader asks, for instance, after reading Mark 1:1, "Who is this Jesus Christ anyway?" Now this may be how a literary theorist might construe the process of reading, but two questions immediately emerge: Did Mark intend such a question? Were not his readers already fully aware of who Jesus was? The fact is that, if the tradition-critical process has taught us anything, it is that the Gospels were written by believers for believers. If this is the case, then any notion of a "tabula rasa" will probably lead to misreadings.

A final criticism is the response to the accusation, at times even cynical,[21] made by literary critics who contend that traditional scholarship (the historical-critical method) is concerned almost exclusively with pre- and extratextual factors, that it excavates Jewish religion in comparison with other religions, or that it seeks Jesus and not the depiction of Jesus. Indeed, there are literally thousands of minute investigations into the nature, extent, and theology of the hypothetical source Q (even debate about the origin of the siglum Q itself!)—most of which never address the issue of the texts of Matthew and Luke.

---

21. Alter, *Biblical Narrative*, 48–49.

The issue is not a simple either/or but revolves around the ultimate goal of one's tradition-critical investigation. It is much more reasonable to contend that the ultimate goal of scholars needs to be shifted from pre- and extratextual factors toward the text itself as illuminated by these various methods. If this is the case, the work of Brevard Childs is a conspicuous model of a more complete method: one must aim to interpret the text as we have it in light of how it got that way. It is not a matter of discarding the historical-critical method; rather, it is a matter of exploiting it for the purpose of understanding the text.

In summary, literary criticism, in spite of some brilliant observations about the text, has its share of methodological weaknesses. Until it can answer some hard questions about referentiality and the nature of communication, about how the earliest churches read the texts, and about a method which is consonant with the text's own evolution as well as its own excesses, it will remain an inadequate discipline.

Having said this, however, it is important not to discard the method as useless. Accordingly, we need to look finally at the value of this discipline for Gospel exegesis.

Positive Evaluation of Literary Criticism

There is no doubt that literary criticism has offered many fresh insights into the Gospel texts; further, the discipline has spawned multifarious studies into various facets of the narratives. When a large number of scholars are involved in one area of research, growth in knowledge is inevitable.

Concentration on the text and the author ("narrator," "implied author") is certainly the most important contribution of literary criticism. The face-to-face stance of the movement, over against tradition criticism, with respect to analysis of the text as opposed to analysis of what lay behind the text, has forced tradition critics to admit that literary critics have the proper orientation in asking first about the meaning of the text.

Consonant with this development has been a growing concern with, and understanding of, genre and the nature of the Gospels. Though debate on genre has continued since the days of the form critics, this deliberation has taken new turns and new questions are now being asked—particularly about comparisons with other works of literature (both ancient and modern). One can only hope that clearer lines will be drawn in our definitions of a "Gospel" as a result.[22]

Third, literary criticism, in its sensitivity to literary features, has demonstrated the artistic, literary nature of the Gospels and the singular force artistic expression creates. What were once merely geographical locations or temporal comments have become, under closer inspection, literary strategies. Literary critics have demonstrated the undeniable artistic concerns of the narrators of the Gospels and have opened up for contemporary scholars new vistas for exploration. Some (and these are not the only) lucid examples of literary design are N. R. Petersen's demonstration of the conscious analogy Luke makes between Jesus and Paul in Luke and Acts,[23] E. S. Malbon's development of "narrative space" in Mark,[24] the explanation of character development by D. Rhoads and D. Michie,[25] and V. K. Robbins's comparison of literary conventions in Jewish and Graeco-Roman literature in order to highlight the Markan depiction of the relationship of Jesus and the disciples.[26] Even if the student disagrees with historical scepticism and literary strategies, these recent treatments will stimulate thought in literary categories—and this will be a gain since the Gospels are literary deposits of the early church.

Finally, literary critics have emphasized the importance of entering into the world of the narrator, accepting his viewpoint and reading from his presuppositions. Since the rise of historical scepticism, conservatives have contended for the importance of accepting an author's presuppositions. On the historical Jesus front, this

---

22. See C. H. Talbert, *What Is a Gospel? The Genre of the Canonical Gospels* (Philadelphia: Fortress, 1977); P. L. Shuler, *A Genre for the Gospels: The Biographical Character of the Gospels* (Philadelphia: Fortress, 1982); Robbins, *Jesus the Teacher;* D. E. Aune, "The Problem of the Genre of the Gospels: A Critique of C. H. Talbert's *What Is a Gospel?*" in *Gospel Perspectives 2: Studies in History and Tradition in the Four Gospels,* ed. by R. T. France and D. Wenham, 9–60 (Sheffield: JSOT, 1981).

23. *Literary Criticism,* 83–86.

24. *Narrative Space and Mythic Meaning in Mark* (San Francisco: Harper & Row, 1986).

25. See *Mark.*

26. See *Jesus the Teacher.*

has been recently expressed by Royce Gruenler[27] and it is now being revived from a literary angle. Though many of these studies are not concerned with the questions of truth and reliability of the Gospel records, they are calling for a more forthright acceptance of the author's viewpoint in order to understand the meaning of the text. This is an important reminder to a generation which has suffered greatly under positivistic historiography. The words of Sternberg are apt: "And whether or not interpreters share this belief, they cannot make proper sense of the narrative *unless they take the narrator's own omniscience as an institutional fact and his demonstration of God's omniscience as a* [sic] *informing principle.*"[28]

The final word about literary criticism, with its divergent concerns and conclusions, is not yet available. The next decade will probably see a fully developed "poetics of Gospel narrative" but that attempt will need to deal with some serious methodological problems if it is to outlive its distant cousin, the historical-critical method.

Suggestions for the Use of Literary Criticism

It will be no surprise to the reader if I conclude on a negative note. Though literary criticism has forced traditional scholarship to rethink some old issues and methods, it is still a discipline fraught with methodological problems. And, until more careful analyses of reference and historical intention are completed, literary criticism will remain a "trend" and will not become a "standard method" for generations to come.

In fact, much of the good in literary criticism has already been exposed through redaction criticism in its "composition criticism" emphases. Granted, the terms were absent and the tack was slightly different, but it cannot be denied that composition critics were thinking in *both* tradition-critical and literary terms. Literary criticism has its place in synoptic exegesis but only as a facet of the tradition-critical process, namely, the concern with the composition

---

27. *New Approaches to Jesus and the Gospels* (Grand Rapids: Baker, 1982), 135–243.
28. *Poetics*, 90; emphasis added.

of the entire work. This subordination of literary criticism has important implications, for it is thereby absorbed into tradition-critical analysis and is not a challenge to it. In conclusion, the importance of literary criticism for synoptic exegesis is its calling attention to the compositional devices which the redactor used as he put the entire Gospel together. What are the kinds of things the exegete must look for in seeking for literary strategies?

First, one needs to understand and appreciate the terms of literary criticism and learn to read the Gospels using such categories. The notion of the "omniscience, omnipotence, and omnipresence" of the implied author and the author's point of view in a narrative are interesting ideas and help explain how a text operates the way it does.

Second, in reading the Gospel narratives, the exegete needs to look for literary devices, such as foreshadowing, chiasm, and inclusion. Foreshadowing, as the term suggests, anticipates later components of a narrative, as when Luke anticipates the rejection of Christ in his programmatic structuring of the inaugural sermon of Jesus in Nazareth (Luke 4:16–30). Chiasm is the repetition of something in reverse order, as in Matthew 7:6 (dogs-swine-swine-dogs). Inclusion is the beginning of a section with an expression or term and the completion of that section with the same expression or term to signal its consummation. Many scholars have patterned Matthew 5:1–9:34 by noting the inclusion of 4:23 and 9:35. The devices of literature are numerous but, with a little familiarity, most students can detect them.[29]

Third, larger literary issues need to be observed. We need to ask questions about the characters, about the relationship of settings with characters, about the plot and how the author puts his story together. Is there development in opposition between Jesus and the Jewish leaders as the story unfolds? Do the disciples gradually break through into the light as Mark's narrative proceeds? How does the record of John the Baptist affect the record of Jesus in Luke and how, in turn, does the record of Jesus affect the record of Paul in Acts? These literary patterns are important for the serious exegete.

---

29. See Lohr, "Oral Techniques," 403–35; Rhoads and Michie, *Mark*, 45–62; Petersen, *Literary Criticism*, 49–92.

In doing literary criticism, the exegete must use a synopsis and not neglect the development of a given tradition. Further, a sharper profile will be obtained as one examines literary strategies in the light of the tradition-critical process, for one will be observing what the author is doing to the traditions (composition criticism).

Selected Bibliography

The following bibliography cites twenty essential introductory works on the synoptic Gospels. For each Gospel, at least two commentaries are recommended: a standard critical study and an evangelical presentation. Additional sources are recommended throughout the text.

History of Gospel Studies

Kümmel, W. G. *The New Testament: The History of the Investigation of Its Problems*. Translated by S. M. Gilmour and H. C. Kee. Nashville: Abingdon, 1972.

Neill, S. *The Interpretation of the New Testament, 1861–1961*. The Firth Lectures, 1962. New York: Oxford University Press, 1966.

Tradition Analysis

Blomberg, C. L. *The Historical Reliability of the Gospels*. Downers Grove, Ill.: Inter-Varsity Press, 1987.

Bultmann, R. *The History of the Synoptic Tradition*. Translated by J. Marsh. New York: Harper & Row, 1963.

Collins, R. F. *Introduction to the New Testament*. Garden City: Doubleday, 1983.

Moule, C. F. D. *The Birth of the New Testament*. 3d ed. San Francisco: Harper & Row, 1981.

Perrin, N. *Rediscovering the Teaching of Jesus*. New York: Harper & Row, 1967.

Stein, R. H. *The Synoptic Problem: An Introduction*. Grand Rapids: Baker, 1987.

Streeter, B. H. *The Four Gospels: A Study of Origins*. London: Macmillan, 1964.

Motif Analysis and Teachings of Jesus

Jeremias, J. *New Testament Theology: The Proclamation of Jesus*. Translated by J. Bowden. New York: Charles Scribner's, 1971.

Marshall, I. H. *Luke: Historian and Theologian*. Grand Rapids: Zondervan, 1970.

Martin, R. P. *Mark: Evangelist and Theologian*. Grand Rapids: Zondervan, 1972.

Meyer, B. F. *The Aims of Jesus*. Philadelphia: Fortress, 1979.

Stanton, G. N., ed. *The Interpretation of Matthew*. Vol. 3, Issues in Religion and Theology. Philadelphia: Fortress, 1983.

Commentaries

Matthew

Carson, D. A. *Matthew*. Vol. 8, Expositor's Bible Commentary. Grand Rapids: Zondervan, 1984; or France, R. T. *The Gospel According to Matthew: An Introduction and Commentary*. Tyndale New Testament Commentary. Grand Rapids: Eerdmans, 1985.

Sabourin, L. *The Gospel According to St. Matthew*. 2 vols. Bandra, Bombay: St. Paul Publications, 1982.

Mark

Lane, W. L. *The Gospel According to Mark*. New International Commentary on the New Testament. Grand Rapids: Eerdmans, 1974.

Taylor, V. *The Gospel According to St. Mark*. London: Macmillan, 1966.

Luke

Fitzmyer, J. A. *The Gospel According to Luke.* 2 vols. Anchor Bible. Garden City: Doubleday, 1983, 1985.

Marshall, I. H. *The Gospel of Luke.* New International Greek Testament Commentary. Grand Rapids: Eerdmans, 1978.